D0937997

Shaping Our Future

SHAPING
OUR FUTURE

Challenges for the Church
in the Twenty-First Century

J. Stephen Freeman, editor

COWLEY PUBLICATIONS
Cambridge ✦ Boston
Massachusetts

Published in the United States of America by Cowley Publications,
a division of the Society of St. John the Evangelist.
No portion of this book may be reproduced, stored in or introduced into a retrieval
system, or transmitted, in any form or by any means—including photocopying—without the prior written permission of Cowley Publications, except in the case of brief
quotations embodied in critical articles and reviews.

Library of Congress Cataloging in Publication Data:
Shaping our future: challenges for the Church in the twenty-first century /
edited by J. Stephen Freeman.
p.   cm.
Papers presented at the Shaping Our Future symposium held in St. Louis, Aug. 1993
ISBN: 1-56101-102-9   cloth (alk. paper)
ISBN: 1-56101-097-9   paper (alk. paper)
1. Pastoral theology—Episcopal Church—Congresses. 2. Episcopal
Church—Congresses. 3. Mission of the church—Congresses.
4. Christianity—Forecasting—Congresses.
I. Freeman, J. Stephen.
BX5820.S53   1994
250—dc20   94-12570

This book is printed on recycled, acid-free paper and was produced in the United
States of America.

Scripture quotations are taken from the *New Revised Standard Version* of the Bible.

Grateful thanks are due to Holly Forman for her assistance in preparing the typescript
and to Cynthia Shattuck of Cowley Publications for her advice and guidance.

This manuscript was copyedited by Cynthia Shattuck and typeset by Vicki Black.
Cover design by Vicki Black.

Cowley Publications
28 Temple Place
Boston, Massachusetts 02111

Contents

Foreword

FROM THE 1991 ANNUAL convention of the diocese of East Tennessee came a resolution calling for action to put forth a plan of structural change that would prepare the church for mission in the twenty-first century. The resolution was rather specific in some areas, and, frankly, it did not speak to my understanding of the church. As a former member of the executive council of the Episcopal Church and chair of its planning and development committee, I knew that progress was being made already in the normal channels of the General Convention and through other interim bodies. The overwhelming vote and concern expressed on the floor of our convention, however, would not let this idea drop.

The bishop and council received the resolution, and I appointed a committee to study what we might do. The Rev. Dr. Jon Shuler was appointed as chair. In the fall of 1992 Dr. Shuler came back with a plan, asking the council for a grant to begin the work. The plan was simple. A forum would be called asking church historians, theologians, and management experts to gather in a place with other church people to discuss the resolution at hand. No more than two hundred people were expected to participate.

Obviously, the idea grew, with encouragement from outside the diocese. In the course of the next several months I informed the Presiding Bishop and the president of the House of Deputies what was going to take place. The proposed gathering was no longer a simple forum of experts but an invitation to any who wanted to be present for a symposium in a central part of the country, St. Louis, in August. Everything was against the symposium: not enough time, floods in St. Louis, critics of doom, and financial woes. Symposium organizers, already overwhelmed with their own professions and ministries, were frustrated in trying to gather a representative group of speakers.

Yet, St. Louis happened. I shall always be grateful that we had the symposium. There is still the wonder and awe that a moderate-sized diocese, at that time the youngest diocese among the domestic dioceses, should produce a well-run and significant opportunity for one thousand Episcopalians to gather in one place to listen, discuss, and above all to worship together. All was made available. The open-space technology brought persons together who would never have known each other. The registration showed a great number of the dioceses represented from a cross section of the church. We were reminded that we were not really grassroots several times, but we looked like most parishes on Sunday mornings. Thirty-some bishops joined me in the closing celebration on Sunday morning in just one worship event that will always remind me of the basic work of the church in her liturgy.

The East Tennessee Initiative has now evolved into Shaping Our Future, Inc., and has a new steering committee and executive board made up of people who live throughout the country. We pass on this mantle to them and pray that they will remember the basics with which we started out. I commend this book to every churchperson. The authors represent some of the best minds of the church today, and as you will see, a variety of opinions.

Jon C. Shuler

Introduction

THIS BOOK IS the direct result of the ministry of ordinary men and women in the Episcopal Church. It has flowed from their attempt to be faithful to the calling of their Lord, and it has flowed from hearts that have sometimes been broken with grief over the current confusion and uncertainty in the community they love. Most of all it is the direct result of the courage of its editor, J. Stephen Freeman, whose brave obedience to the Holy Spirit in 1991 set in motion a chain of events that have helped to call the church to an era of major systemic change and, it is to be hoped, biblical reform.

Many concerned voices have been raised for years, but the tide of those who questioned this church's clarity concerning its life and mission reached a new crest when the Shaping Our Future symposium was held in St. Louis during the summer of 1993. Few believed that over one thousand people would come together, at their own expense, to discuss this church's structure and mission for the twenty-first century. That they did is directly owing to the previous presentation in Knoxville in 1991, of what has come to be called "The Freeman Resolution." The story of the connection between these two events is the background to this collection of essays.

Almost no one would have imagined in advance that the seventh convention of the diocese of East Tennessee would rise above the ordinary business of an ordinary diocese. But it did the moment Stephen Freeman walked to the microphone to present his resolution calling for the restructuring of the church. Behind the scenes most people expected the matter quickly to be defeated. There was even an attempt to kill the resolution in committee, but it was courageously rescued by another young priest of the diocese. When the floor debate be-

gan it was immediately clear that the substance of the resolution had touched a real nerve, as person after person rose to
speak. Almost no one spoke in favor of every part of the proposal, but what became abundantly clear to most observers
was that nearly everyone thought that something in the
church was "broken." There was little agreement about *what*,
but near unanimity that it was time for a change.

Well over an hour of debate produced much heat and little
light, and the resolution was referred—without a vote on its
merits—to the bishop and council for consideration and resub-
mission at the next diocesan convention. Few realized then
that the matter had thus been postponed for fifteen months,
since there was no convention scheduled for 1992.

A new diocesan bishop presided at the next meeting of the
council, and after preliminary reports he announced that a sub-
committee to handle the Freeman Resolution was to be
formed, and that I was to be the chairman! Little did Bishop
Tharp—nor I—realize how far that decision would eventually
reach.

I accepted the bishop's appointment, but only after private
discussion in which I reminded him of my own friendship
with Stephen Freeman and of my conviction that his resolution was of immense importance to the future well-being of
the Episcopal Church. My own parochial experience and theological reflection upon it had long since convinced me that the
church was in the midst of a major systemic collapse, and that
without significant restructuring for mission and ministry our
future was bleak indeed. To Bishop Tharp's lasting credit, he
reiterated his desire for me to serve in the task he had outlined,
and so we went forward.

The early work of the committee was very discouraging, to
say the least, as it became bogged down in the variety of opinions and presuppositions held by the members who had been
appointed. Many of us thought the work would never bear
fruit, as we were hopelessly stuck in contrary ideas. It was
then that Stephen Freeman, once again, served us all by an act
of independent obedience. He wrote an article which *The Living
Church* published in June of 1992 and which gathered up the

substance of his resolution. That article proved to be the fuse to a large explosion.

From around the nation, responses to the article poured in. Father Freeman and Bishop Tharp began to receive phone calls and letters, all of which indicated that there was a very real excitement about the substance of the proposal that was being put forward. Further, it seemed to many that the East Tennessee provenance of the resolution was a great strength. We were perceived as a centrist diocese, in the heartland of the country, and that commended the work to many observers.

When the committee next assembled, in August of 1992, the notoriety of our work excited us, but still our differences concerning the original resolution had us deadlocked. It was in this meeting, however, that the proposal to hold a national symposium first emerged. What if we temporarily tabled the resolution but came up with a plan to discuss the entire subject with anyone who was interested? From that moment, the symposium was born.

At first we had no idea how large the event would become, nor did we see the enormity of the task of facilitating it, but we were at last united about what to do. Bishop Tharp consulted with seventeen other bishops, the Presiding Bishop, and many others throughout the church before settling on the dates of August 12-15, 1993, in St. Louis, Missouri. We were underway, though none of us could possibly imagine how thrilling and challenging would be the ride.

The shape of the symposium developed slowly at first, but soon took on a life of its own. We decided to pose several questions to the church to focus our purpose and the responses of those who would participate. For example, "Do our current structures aid or impede the spread of the kingdom of God? If not, why not, and what can we do about it?" Another recurring question was this: "Is the Episcopal Church organized in such a way that it can be effective in mission and ministry in the twenty-first century?"

Invitations to speak went out, many to people some would not have considered to be "appropriate" because we had determined it would be helpful to invite people who were outsiders to the Episcopal family as well as those who knew us well. To this decision we owe some of the most stimulating thought contained in this collection of essays, as well as much of the exciting energy at the symposium itself. We were later criticized by some because of the perceived "incorrectness" of our speaker list, but from the beginning we were concerned to ask people we believed could address the subject with a fresh approach.

We were told early on that we did not have the expertise, time, or money to do what needed to be done. Our critics were right on all three counts. But our perseverance came from the growing conviction that we had been called by God to the task. We began to pray in earnest, and to call others to pray, that we would be able to discern the right and be given the courage to perform it. We offered all that we had, and that was enough.

As the symposium opened over one thousand people were gathered from ninety-three dioceses and five nations. There were thirty-seven bishops and more than one hundred deputies to the next General Convention. There were certainly gaps in the demographic makeup of the assembly, but it was abundantly clear that the participants represented the grassroots leadership of the Episcopal Church. And from the opening service of worship to the concluding blessing four days later, there was an air of expectation and excitement. The essays you are about to read, however worthy, cannot capture that mood, but the context in which they were given needs to be remembered.

When the time came to return to our homes, a sense of great anticipation seemed to hover over the convention hall as a question rose in many minds: "Now what?" The symposium had developed a life of its own, and the threads of many presentations seemed to be weaving a coherent whole, but it was not clear to the leadership quite what they needed to do with what had occurred, or if anything was to be done at all. What was clear was that a renewed hope was born in many hearts in St. Louis. I would express it in this way: "There is yet a possibility, under God, that this church we love will be renewed by the grace of Christ Jesus for a great adventure of the Holy Spirit in the twenty-first century."

The book you now hold in your hands gathers up a majority of the papers and principal talks given in St. Louis, and offers them to the whole church for continuing reflection and prayer. Not everyone who spoke is represented in these pages, but we believe these papers deserve to be a part of the permanent record. All the talks remain available on audio and video cassette, however, and can be purchased through the continuing ministry of *Shaping Our Future, Inc.*, in Knoxville, Tennessee.

It was to this latter organization that the work of the East Tennessee Initiative was bequeathed, and it has been incorporated as a nonprofit religious corporation under the laws of the state of Tennessee. It has adopted as its mission: "To work for the biblical reform of the Episcopal Church for effective mission and ministry in the twenty-first century." In October of 1993 I resigned as rector of the Church of the Ascension, Knoxville, to become president of this new ministry.

What then of the future of the Episcopal Church? As speaker after speaker pointed out in St. Louis, the answer to this question is known only to God. What this collection of essays makes plain, however, is that a season of reformation is breaking over this community. It has come unexpectedly to many and belatedly to some, but come it has. To many of us it seems true that "this is the Lord's doing and it is marvelous in our eyes." If this is so, we are *all* going to be challenged by the unexpected movement of the Holy Spirit of God, and we are *all* going to be called to repentance and renewed faith.

When the Shaping Our Future symposium began in St. Louis, the flooding in the midwestern states had reached devastating proportions. In the midst of that surrounding flood, we were assembled to seek to discern the wisdom of God for his church. It was Loren Mead who first likened our task to that of the disciples of old, when a storm on the Sea of Galilee threatened to flood their boat and sink them beneath the waters. Their Lord and Master came to them on the troubled waters and led them to safety on the shore. He called Peter to come to him on the troubled waters, and Peter came. Now Jesus calls to us as well, and as of old it requires faith to get out of the boat.

May this collection of essays be part of God's plan to call you to walk with him through the present storm. May you, and all the whole church, once again surrender to his most gracious will. May it be so for us all, and may it be to the honor and glory of his Holy Name revealed to us in Jesus.

Part One

The Challenge of Structure

T wenty years ago a question about structure (much less *church* structure) would have stirred little interest outside the boardrooms of corporate America. However, with the end of the Cold War and the pressures of a growing global economy, *how* we structure ourselves to accomplish any task has become the stuff of daily conversation. Governments, corporations, organizations of every sort have begun to ask very similar questions of themselves. The church is no stranger to this conversation. The symposium in St. Louis, one of the largest gatherings of laity and clergy in Episcopal Church history, was occasioned by a discussion of structure. The presentations included in this first section demonstrate why this conversation has generated so much interest. It is a conversation which asks questions of the very heart of the church's life and mission. The authors included in this section disagree over the relative importance of church structure itself, and some would argue that structure is but a subset of the larger question of mission. None, however, dismiss it as of no importance. How we structure ourselves for mission can be as crucial as the mission itself.

Loren Mead, founder and president of the Alban Institute, has long been a familiar figure in discussions of "how to do church." For years he has been one of the primary researchers, authors, and consultants for those seeking help for troubled churches, or for those who were seeking merely to understand the church. His talk, "The Parish Church and Tomorrow," draws on some of his most recent work, including material published in *Transforming Congregations for the Future* (Washington, D.C.: Alban Institute, 1994). Part sermon, part analysis, it offers a straightforward picture of the "storm" which is troubling the church and a challenge to "get out of the boat" and get on with the mission of the gospel.

Robert Jenson, an ordained Lutheran minister, is on the faculty of St. Olaf's College in Northfield, Minnesota. He is recognized around the world as one of the most prominent figures in American theology today. He was previously Lutheran World Federation Lecturer in Theology and Chaplain to Lutherans at Oxford University. His many works include *The Triune Identity: The Christian Interpretation of God; America's Theologian: A Recommendation of Jonathan Edwards;* and *The Unbaptized God: The Basic Flaw in Ecumenical Theology.* The lecture included in this section came in answer to an invitation to place the question of church structure in the classical context of the doctrine of the Trinity. More than a discussion of structure, his essay is a masterful exposition of the cornerstone doctrine of Christian faith. It is a reminder of the serious challenges facing the church's theology in the coming century as well as a resounding affirmation that classical theology is sufficient to meet those challenges.

Stephen Freeman, author of the original article that gave rise to the symposium in St. Louis, is rector of St. Stephen's Episcopal Church in Oak Ridge, Tennessee. His forum presentation develops both his earlier historical analysis and theological demands for structural reform. He argues that structures created in the image of the corporate world are unsuited to the task of forming Christian community. His central question is of the character of the church: "What kind of people are we called to be?" It is a question that lies at the heart of the challenge discussed in this section, how we structure the church.

Loren Mead

The Parish Church and Tomorrow

IT IS INTERESTING to be in St. Louis, with the crest of the wave going down the river. We've all been reading about that high water. Last Sunday we read a lesson about Jesus *walking* on the water, and that is the background for what I want to talk about today. Before I get into my discursus on last Sunday's gospel, I have a couple of private words to say to you. The first thing I want to say about our structural problem is that it is bigger than we are. The issue of church structure is related to something God is doing throughout this world. The issue of how you build community, of how you come together, is being thought out in Russia, in Yugoslavia. If you go to Somalia, you will see what happens if there are no structures. If you look at the business world or the business page of your paper, you will see what is happening to IBM, AT&T, and General Motors. Structural issues are interfering with life. God is calling us to new life in many different places. We have structural problems, but those problems are part of something larger than we are.

The second thing I want to say is that although we are struggling with our structures, they themselves are not the real issue. *Structure* in the church has always flowed from what we understood the *mission* of the church to be. *Structure* is the way we try to put ourselves together to do *mission*. When our understanding of mission and the way we structure ourselves get crosswise to one another, we have trouble. Well, this is "River City" and "we got trouble in River City." I have the same distress as that mentioned by almost everyone who has been on this podium. Somewhere in the media this meeting has been called a "meeting of dissidents." I am not a dissident. I love the church that has nurtured me, frustrated me, but also stood behind me all my life.

As I speak with you tonight, I am holding in honor a long list of people who have given of themselves to this church and made my ministry possible. As you go through these next few days I am hoping you will be making your list, too, remembering the people who have lived in the church and who, through the structures—good, bad, and indifferent—have ministered to you and to the world. I celebrate the extraordinary gifts that have been passed to you and to me through the very structures with which we have problems. I join you tonight in thinking that our task is to strengthen mission rather than focusing on structures. I am not interested in structures. I am not interested in restructuring or organizing. I am not interested in fixing or changing structures. I am interested in the church's mission. I am interested in what God is calling us to be and to do. I think we need to figure out how to *work* on those things together—*that* is the question of structure—and that comes second. That is why I am here. To work on mission.

Having said that now, I get to the second part of my speech. The gospel story I have in mind was read in our churches last Sunday. This gospel is a simple story. The disciples are in a boat and a big storm comes up. Jesus is on the shore catching up on his prayers, and he walks out to the boat when he finishes. In Mark, he walks beside the boat and goes over to the other side to meet the disciples. Mark likes Jesus to keep things kind of secret. But in Matthew, Jesus walks straight to the boat, the disciples see him, and they are scared to death. "What is this—a ghost?" Jesus calms them down a bit but the waves are pretty high. Peter says, "Hey, I'm coming to you! Can I come walk to you?" Jesus says, "Sure, come on!" Peter steps out there and suddenly sees the waves. Something else happened then which I will tell you about later. The Bible doesn't tell you about it, but I know it. I know it because I have experienced it. Anyway, Peter gets scared and Jesus grabs him and helps him back into the boat. You know the story. That is the framework for what I want to talk about.

The first thing I want to talk about is what Peter and the disciples felt when they saw Jesus coming. They were not only afraid of this ghost, they were scared of the storm. I want to talk about the storm that you and I are in. Let's pretend that this is a boat—this place. We have a few more than he had in his boat, but it is still rocking, and there is a storm out there. We're afraid. I want to talk about some parts of the storm we have become accustomed to. One part of the storm, which I wrote about in my book, *The Once and Future Church*, is that our model of what we are trying to do has changed. If structure should come out of our sense of mission, then one of our problems is that our sense of mission has changed. That is part of the storm we are in. We have come to understand and articulate mission differently.

Although it is an oversimplification, we can label the society in which we were young "Christendom." We understood all of society to be Christian. We, in our parishes, were in the midst of a Christian society. We understood life that way. The missionary frontier was far away from us. You could see it way out on the outskirts of society. It was the faraway places, the "way off mission." We did not have a sense of an immediate presence of mission in our parishes. The people in our parishes did not participate in mission themselves. They were not responsible for it. The people who were on a *mission* were the folks who were on the edge, somewhere outside of Christendom. They were largely professional people whom we hired, and we in our parishes had the task of supporting that mission. We raised the money. We raised our children to go into that mission. We prayed for that mission. Remember mite boxes? They were important because the money went to support the mission of the church. But the mission was not something that was done by us. It was something in the charge of the professionals.

This model of mission is what we grew up in and it is this model of mission that our institutions and structures were built to support. However, some years ago we began discovering that our understanding of mission has changed. The missionary frontier that used to be far away is now right on our doorstep. Today missionary action is based *in the parish* and ministers to the community immediately surrounding it. That is a very different kind of mission, and calls for a different kind of activity and a different kind of structure. Whereas in the Christendom model ministry and mission were something you could hire somebody to do and support, in the mission model that is developing today *everybody* in the congregation is a part of the mission. Our structures reflect an old sense of mission and have not been adjusted to fit the new situation. I would say that in Christendom our concern became how to develop an apostolic ministry, and everybody knew what that "ministry" meant. "Ministry" meant the people with collars. In the world we confront today we are talking about trying to develop an apostolic *church* where every member is an apostle, "one who is sent out." It is not the professionals who are the ministry, it is all of us.

One way of looking at the structures and what has happened to them is to use this distinction between building an apostolic ministry and building an apostolic church. For example, the way you structure yourself for apostolic *ministry* (the Christendom model) is that you have parishes which provide resources for dioceses which provide resources for the national church which decides where the mission needs to be attacked. Please note that all of this is driven by a desire to do mission. We built structures to do mission, not to please people in New York or in diocesan headquarters or in parish offices. Those structures were built to channel resources to mission.

In the model of an apostolic *church* (post-Christendom) the mission action is primarily local. The need is right at home, around the parish. The flow of resources has got to be toward that mission. However, we have not yet learned to do that well. Another problem remains, because there is still another mission need that is far off. In our enthusiasm for the local mission frontier, we are sometimes being a little shortsighted, forgetting about that other mission frontier. But this illustrates the structural differences between building apostolic ministry and building an apostolic church. It is a larger task. The focus of our mission is part of the storm we are in, but there is more to the storm than that.

Some of you may be statistically minded and some not, but I got started on a quest for knowledge one day when I saw a curve on a graph in a diocesan paper. The curve showed a steep downward decline, while the headline over this curve was, "Statistics show the Episcopal Church is growing." I looked at it carefully. As it turned out, the last bit of the graph showed that there were three thousand more baptized people in the Episcopal Church in 1990 than there had been the previous year. As a matter of fact, in 1992 there were forty thousand more baptized members. Unfortunately, those who keep the statistics changed the definitions so that we cannot be sure we are counting the same thing each year. Nevertheless, the direction of the curve for a number of years has been decidedly down. And all of the mainline churches—the Presbyterians, the Methodists, the Congregationalists—are showing a similar pattern of decline.

Point one of this is that whatever is going on here is not simply going on with us. The issue is larger than we are. The storm is larger than the Episcopal Church. However, there is worse news. The statistical curve for the Episcopal Church does not include what is happening to the general population. In the context of the population's increase, the Episcopal Church has not experienced a mere dip in its membership, but a nosedive. If you look at the population and how we are doing in the potential (pardon the expression) "market," then we are not doing well at all, and the same is true of the other denominations I have mentioned. This nosedive is part of our storm, and is happening to us for good, bad, and indifferent reasons. You can argue with statistics—you know how inaccurate the statistics are in the parochial reports. But the decline is part of the problem we are in.

A few further facts. Episcopalians were about 1.7 percent of the U.S. population for a number of years. In fact, we went above that from 1945 to 1965. We prospered, then dropped down. What happened in the churches between 1945 and 1965? How many of your dioceses built diocesan headquarters during those years? I bet a lot of you did. How many of your dioceses started and decided to have diocesan staffs? I bet many of you did. How many of you built "815"? All of us. How many of us started and developed things like industrial missions and the National Council of Churches? A lot of those things were happening in that period, which was an anomalous period in the church. We built structures, some of which we have to reexamine now.

I am afraid that during this anomalous period of unusual growth we became imprinted organizationally. It was during that time that many of us came to understand how to do church. Many of the things we came to understand are going to have to be unlearned if our decline continues. That is part of the problem with our structures. It is part of the problem of the storm we are in. But there is more.

Let me quote from a paper the Rev. Gay Jennings wrote in the diocese of Ohio:

> In 1992, the diocese of Ohio concluded that the bare minimum needed [to employ a full-time seminary-trained priest as well as support building facilities] is between $75,000 and $85,000. That's the magic number. Forty percent of the 111 congregations...have budgets of less than $80,000! In 1982 only seven congregations in the diocese of Ohio were served by clergy on a part-time basis. Today 33 of our congregations...are served either by cluster clergy or bi-vocational clergy.

Financial problems are also part of the storm we are in. Many of your dioceses are struggling with it. Many of the people who are here from parishes are struggling with it, and there have been extraordinary accomplishments in the area of stewardship in the Episcopal Church, more than in most of the other denominations. Efforts such as the Alabama Plan and many others contributed. Some of those were outside the structure. They decided they wanted to do something and they went out and did it. Different groups did it in different ways.

It does not matter how they did it, but a lot of people in our church have become generous givers to the church, more so than in previous years. I think we can be proud of that, but there is a limit. When you have a membership decline such as ours, it means that our givers are getting older and there are fewer of them. They are giving more, but there is a limit. Many places are up against it right now.

There will be congregations next year who will have to ask for grants for the first time in their history. What happens if your medical insurance goes up twenty percent? Presbyterians tell me that the drop in national mission giving is exactly equal to the rise in medical insurance premiums which they have to pay. These things are connected. What happens in a society that is less supportive of the church than it was in the past when taxation issues come up? There are churches represented in this place who have property being taxed that was not being taxed a few years ago. Clergy came very close to losing their housing allowance tax benefit. That may happen one of these days, and when it does it will have further consequences for what it costs to keep a full-time ordained minister in a congregation. This is part of the storm. No wonder Peter was scared and wanted to get back in the boat. You would be smart to be scared of the storm that is out there. There is plenty of tough stuff that we have to face.

As far as the financial side of things goes—and I'm sure that all the clergy here will dislike my saying this—I see no way out now. You cannot change structures without new resources. It is a bunch of romantic poppycock to think that you can really redevelop an institution without investing new resources in that restructuring. I cannot see any way we can face the next fifty years of the church's life without major attention to endowments. I will tell you straight out that your worst enemy will be your clergy, because clergy have a severe lack of faith around money. Many are incompetent around money, and lay people are incompetent to let them get away with it. One of the greatest spiritual problems for everybody in this room is that we are rich people, all of us, and we need help understanding how to live the way we are. Our clergy have not been very helpful. This is an area of growth that we really need some help in. Many of you in this room believe in tithing. I do. If you believe in tithing, everyone of you should have at least ten percent of your estate in trust for the church. I do not care what kind of church or where in the church. But everyone of you ought to have a will with the church figuring very strongly in it.

I will quit meddling now, but I am telling you that there is a storm around the boat and the storm will not be getting better soon. The winds are high. The question is, "Are you willing to get your feet wet?"

Peter responded. Peter got out of the boat. I think we need to get out of the boat. We need to get in the water. We can no longer can hire somebody else to do it. It has got to be us. We cannot ride it out in first class. We have got to get out into the water. What do we need to do this? It is not complicated. What do we need to have the courage to get out? *We need each other in community.* We must get deeper, stronger community in our congregations. Small groups, big groups, better worship, whatever. How vapid much of the community is in our parishes! There are social groups and we are not together in any kind of depth. Community must be at the heart of every parish. We need one another if we are to have the courage to get out and walk on the water.

We need to be grounded in Scripture and the story. We do not even have good Sunday schools for our children! As adults we spend hardly any time studying Scripture, and opportunities to study together are not available. We need to be able to touch base with Jesus. I do that every Tuesday morning at the Eucharist, and for many people in the church the Eucharist is part of their regular life. We must also have a sense of the Spirit truly empowering us to do our work in the world. Where do you get these things? You get them in your parish. That is what a parish is. You have a building and a man or woman who runs it. You have committees and all. I do not care about all that. We need to be empowered. We need to structure ourselves to see that this happens for us, both in our big parishes and in our little parishes, city parishes and country parishes. If we had that, we would be able to get out and walk on the water. If we do not have that we will sit around wondering who is going to get their feet wet. A place to be empowered is what we need. I call that a parish. Maybe you put a lot of structures around it, maybe not.

What does a parish need? For those of you who work in dioceses, let me tell you what parishes need. For those of you in parishes who want to be parochial and congregational, let me tell you what a parish needs. These are things I have found. Parishes need help when they get in trouble. And they do get in trouble. Congregations mess up all the time and they need somebody who will help them. They need to be "jacked up." Many congregations do nothing. They sit around on their hands. They need somebody to come in and say, "What are you doing about mission?" We need somebody from outside, a bishop or someone. Other churches call them other things. Some of you call them something else, too. But parishes need to be "jacked up" when they are off-base.

Congregations need pastoral care. Congregations have terrible tragedies that occur and they need somebody to come in and help them grieve. They have victories, too, and they need somebody to come in and celebrate with them.

Congregations need technical assistance from time to time. Something happens. The community changes rapidly and they do not know how to deal with it and they need somebody to come in and help them understand. They need to change the structures of their life and they need somebody to help them with that. They need help developing, training, and changing leadership. Some parishes do this well, but many parishes lack the people power to do it. They need somebody to come in and help them.

Congregations need affirmation. They need a sense of a larger mission. They need to know that they belong to a world-wide community which is facing the issues of the gospel across the world. That is my definition of a diocese. I do not know how many committees you need to do that work. I do not know how many people you need on a staff. It is complicated work. I have worked at it for twenty years, outside the structures. It is hard to do but congregations need it, and they get sick if they do not have it. If you need structure, there is a framework for it.

If we have all those things, it will help us to get out of the boat. Why do you suppose Peter started sinking? Have you ever tried to get out of the boat? If you take a chance, if you get out of the boat and try to walk on water, people will try to make you sink. I got out twenty years ago. I got out of the Episcopal Church's regular structures because I wanted to build something that worked on the structures. But anybody who messes with these structures and gets out of the boat is going to get hurt.

This is the part of the story that is not in the Scriptures—what Peter heard. People back in the boat said, "Peter! Don't do that! You can't do that until you get your theology straight!" And Peter started wondering about his theology and he started sinking. Then somebody else in the other part of the boat said, "You know, we haven't got our decision-making process clear. Did we delegate him to do that or not?" Peter, wondering if he had the authority to do it, sunk a little deeper in the water.

Another one said, "Look at him sink. I knew it was premature to try something like that." Another one said, "Look at him sink. Serves him right. He's too assertive." Another said, "Peter! Wait! You're not being inclusive. We've got to get somebody from South Palestine!" One said, "Peter, before you do that you need a consultant."

Another one said, "You know, if we could get everybody to tithe, we could all have life jackets." Somebody else said, "You know, we've got to have better small group activities to support somebody who's willing to do something like that." Another said—waiting until after Peter was already out on the water—"Wait a minute. Let's have a prayer first." And, "Young people really aren't in favor of older people taking leadership like that. We ought to consult them first." Another whose voice I know in the back of the boat said, "Well, look at him! We'll never elect *him* bishop!" And then the one that probably would be me said, "Come back here, Peter! Don't be a damn fool! It's wet out there."

You'll hear voices like that, if you are not the one talking. If you decide that you are going to try to make a difference, it is not going to be easy. The storm is raging. A lot of those voices are right. It *is* dangerous out there. Look out for the snake oil salesmen who say it is easy or simple, for it is not easy and it is not simple. But let me tell you this. Peter got out there and he walked. And he walked on water in spite of the storm. The storm that we are in is not going to be over for some generations. We are not going to turn all of this stuff around quickly, and the people who say "We've only got to do this, and we've only got to do that" are wrong. But Jesus reached out to Peter. Remember that.

Now, between you and me. Nobody can walk on water. You know that. I know that. It is stupid to think we can walk on water. The storm is too much. But Jesus reached out to Peter. It is absurd that God expects you and expects our church to walk on water, because the storm is so high and the winds are even higher. Here in St. Louis there is relief now. The crest has gone by. The levees held. I am not going to give you that comfort about the storm we are in. I don't think the crest is here yet and I think it is still raining hard upriver. But his hand is out to you. I ask you to try walking on the water.

I learned a little song from Mother Scott at St. Stephen's Church (with a little change):

> Walk on the water,
>> Walk on the water, children.
> Walk on the water,
>> God's going to trouble the waters.

Remember that. We are going to walk on the waters.

Some years ago I was down at Pawley's Island in South Carolina. My children were also there and one afternoon I was supposed to take care of them. I didn't know what to do with children at the beach, so I went in town to Lachicotte's store. I asked the people there, "I'm going to take my children fishing this afternoon. Is that what you do with children around the beach?"

"Yeah, you can do that, but nothing's biting."

"I've got to do something with them. What do I have to buy?"

The manager sold me a couple of things that you fish with but said, "What you really ought to do is come back in October. That's when the fish really begin to bite."

That afternoon I was walking out with my wife to the south point along the creek. I could see somebody fishing. Fly fishing in salt water! I had never seen that before. Up on the bank there were about four or five cases with flies and stuff hanging out. As I walked up I spoke to the man and said, "Good afternoon. Having any luck?"

He said, "Nope."

I had never seen anybody fishing as hard as he was fishing. I said, "I heard they're not biting much."

He said, "Yep, I know."

I said, "I was over at Lachicotte's store today and they said it was a bad time of year."

"Yep. I know."

I said, "They told me to come back in October. That's when they bite."

Then the guy said, "Yep. But I'm here now."

We do not have the church of fifty years ago. We do not have the church of fifty years from now. We have a church that is in the midst of a great storm. But we have the invitation. And we have the power to get out into the life of that church in this world and walk on water. It is impossible. But Jesus' hand is out.

Robert W. Jenson

The Trinity and
Church Structure

SOMETIMES IT SEEMS RIGHT that even a lecture should have a
text, if not always a biblical text. The topic on which I was
asked to speak, the import of the doctrine of Trinity for the
structure of the church, has been a staple of ecumenical theology for years. We have a repertoire of official and private state-
ments from which to choose. Just so, I thought I might go
right to the top, and take as my text an address of John Paul II
to a delegation from the Bossey Ecumenical Institute in Febru-
ary of last year. Minus pleasantries, exhortations, and proof
texts, the official English translation of the Pope's address ran:

> For Christians the supreme model of communion is the Holy
> Trinity, the mystery of three divine persons in a perfect com-
> munion of love. Every work and deed of Jesus Christ, the incar-
> nate Son of God, was a revelation of the inner life which he
> shares with the Father and the Holy Spirit....In the plan of sal-
> vation God willed to reconcile mankind to himself by making it
> possible for us to participate in this mystery of divine commun-
> ion through his Son....The People of God, made one by sharing
> in the divine unity, is, as the Second Vatican Council says, "a
> sacrament or sign and instrument of intimate union with God
> and of the unity of all humanity."

I will not only make this passage the text of my remarks, I
will try to be faithful to it. Indeed, I will, like the great Scot-
tish preachers, take the sequence of the text's propositions for
my own outline.

So, proposition one. *Christians have been given a "model" of true communion, and this model is the communion that is actual in God, in that God is triune.* In the present situation of the American church, we must begin with the most elementary point of all: the church *does* have a model of communion. If we think the shape of our community could use some work—as some Episcopalians evidently do—we neither need nor are permitted to start from scratch; we are given a model. And this model is not a philosophical anthropology, not even one that makes much of *koinonia* or "I-Thou"; it is not a political or social ideal; and it is assuredly not somebody's guess about what sort of community will best attract the baby-boomers. The model is God.

And the first thing about God is that he is who he is who he is who...and is what he is what he is what he is....It is *we* who are malleable to the agendas we project onto one another, and the very difference between God and us is that he is not. Thus the divine model of communion is sheerly given to us, to be accepted or rejected as is. We indeed have much freedom in shaping our churchly future; this is a point which we Lutherans have made with great and tedious emphasis. But we have no choice at all about the shape to be realized, a point which Lutherans have been reluctant to grant but which Anglicans have straight, or used to have straight. When the church thinks about community, it thinks by a triune model or it is not thinking as the church.

Returning to the words of our text, we are safe, I think, in supposing that when John Paul spoke of a "model" he had a standard patristic and scholastic notion in mind. In the theological and philosophical tradition, a model or archetypical image is doubly related to that of which it is the model. Something's archetype is, first, the ground of its being, and, second, revealed through it.

Thus our text says first that God's triunity is the ground of the church's structured being. We have no decisions to make at this level. The church simply *has* a triune structure, because God has decided to have this particular created analogue of his own being. And our text says second that God's triunity is to be revealed by the church's structured being. Here is our as-

signment in the matter. As we make or unmake offices, feed or
starve bureaucracies, establish or terminate programs, we are
given one and only one criterion. We are so to work on the
shape of the church that when the world sees the church it
need not squint to see the triunity of God.

Proposition two. *We can take the triune communal life for our
model because we do in fact know it.* We know the triune communal life in that we are in human converse with one of its members, the incarnate Son. And that is to say we know the triune
life because we are ourselves involved in it, for we know and
are involved in the story of Jesus the Christ, which *is* the story
of one triune member's activity with the other two. In Pope
John Paul's language, as we hear Jesus' words and see his deeds
we are seeing and hearing the inner triune life of God; therefore, we do not need to figure out what real communion
would be like. Nor, when told that God is the model of real
communion, do we need to peer for him through the metaphysical distances, to capture intimations and glimpses with
our metaphors and figures of speech. We need only heed the
gospel that is spoken among us, for it is a direct narrative account of the divine communal life.

Such christological audacity is hard for us. It is utterly in-
consistent with our ideologies: it is a flat-out claim to know
the true and the good, and tramples brutally on individual
epistemological autonomy. The gospel, if taken to be true, is
the mother of all hegemonic meta-narratives. Probably neither
the Episcopalians nor the Lutherans are any longer capable of
saying anything quite so Christian as the Pope said, that "every
word and deed of Jesus Christ, the incarnate Son of God, was a
revelation of the inner life which he shares with the Father and
the Holy Spirit." Indeed, much contemporary pop-theology is
passionate to insist that no revelation can give us more than,
as one document of my denomination put it, "glimpses of the
divine."

But if we think that the pusillanimous christology current in
America is the truth, then this conference should in reason
pack up and go home, for the course of events is then utterly
predictable. Then we have nothing by which to guide our

shaping of churchly futures but our ideological preferences and sociological best guesses. There will be as many of these as there are parties and participants. And after you have gone home each party will promote its agenda as before. Only if it is true—that the words and deeds of Christ are those of the Son living from and with the Father, so that hearing and seeing the words and deeds of Christ we observe God's own inner communal life—can the church know any model of community that transcends our sundry ideological urges and so might free us to transcend them here.

These elementary points made, we do of course want to go on to more substantive considerations. We want to do more than simply insist that the triune life is the church's model of communion. We want to describe at least some features of a communion based on that model, and to do that we need to develop some features of the doctrine of Trinity itself.

Our text presumes a doctrine of Trinity without describing it. Since it is a patriarch of the West speaking, we may expect that the Pope has in mind a trinitarian doctrine of a generally Western type, and where the text gives no other indication I will presume Western teaching. But it also seems that something more interesting is afoot. It is, according to our text, a triune *life* that is God. And this life is constituted in the *community* of persons who can and do *love* each other, that is, it is a community of persons in the full modern sense of conscious and willing subjects. Our text transcends the Western tendency to think only of the one triune God as personal in this sense, and to take the inner being of God as a closed mystery which, whatever it may be, is surely not lively or communal.

Moreover, what Jesus' words and deeds reveal, according to our text, is Jesus' own action as himself one member of the triune life. Western trinitarian theology has often wanted to protect the inner being of God from contamination by temporality, and has tried to do this by building a metaphysical wall between the immanent Trinity and the economic Trinity. Not so here. The earthly career of Jesus reveals, as the action of one agent of God's immanent triune life, not the sheer "procession" of a *Logos* as such, but the incarnate Jesus' own participation in the triune life.

This divine community, in our text, is a perfect love between differentiated persons. The last point first. The Father is not the Son nor is the Son the Spirit nor is the Spirit the Father. Only the Father is the *fons trinitatis*; only the Son is the Father's Word; only the Spirit is the Freedom of the Father and the Son—and so on, for as long as anyone may wish to pursue the dialectic. Every work of the Trinity is done by the one triune God, but this does not mean that each triune person does the same thing. A work of God is a work of the one triune God precisely in that each person performs his distinct triune role in the doing of it; as the Cappadocian summary rule had it, each work comes from the Father, is carried out in the Son, and is perfected by the Spirit. But our text's great point about these persons is that they perfectly love one another. That is, each of them finds himself in what the other receives from him.

The negative first. The differentiation of the divine persons is no kind of autonomy; none of the divine three claims any rights from the others. The three are lovers, and so genuine free doers of a life together. But that does not mean what we are likely to take it to mean, that each is free also *from* the others. Rather, as the great scholastics teach us, there is each of the three only in that he is with and for and from the other two: *"persona...divina significat relationem...per modum substantiae"* (ST I, q.29, art.4). According to St. Thomas, it is the very divinity of a divine person that he has no subsistence other than his relation to the other divine persons. Father, Son, and Spirit, we may say, are infinitely co-dependent.

And finally on this line, the differentiation of persons is hierarchical. To be sure, the traditional hierarchy, constituted by the *monarchia* of the Father, by the one-way traffic of the relations of origin, may not be the only hierarchy in God. Some contemporaries, like myself, think we can descry other triune hierarchies, perhaps one constituted by a procession of liberty from the Spirit to the Son and the Father. But however that may be, the triune life is not egalitarian. If it is democratic—and the previous considerations may indeed suggest use of this word—the divine democracy is the sort of "organic" democracy envisioned by such American thinkers as Horace Bushnell.

Now for proposition three. God's act to reconcile us to himself is nothing so uninteresting as forgiving us or liberating us or empowering us simply as some of his creatures out here. *God reconciles us by taking us into himself, into the community that he himself lives as Father and Son and Spirit.* Here there are centuries of puny theology to forget. God's reconciliation is not just that he makes us better human creatures. He will make us perfect human creatures, and he will do so by incorporating us as additional personal subjects of his own life—as the whole church once had the courage to say, by "deifying" us. The difference between the average god and the triune God is that the latter has *room* in himself, and so has room in himself for others than himself if he so wills. As my next most honored theological hero after Gregory of Nyssa, Jonathan Edwards, once put it with perfect "second naiveté," there is a sort of familial society in God, and it is God's purpose to bring redeemed humankind into that family as the daughter-in-law.

Humanity's destiny is to live in a community of perfect love between differentiated persons. This love is generatively enacted as the love of the Father and the Son and the Spirit. But we will live amidst this love precisely as we are communally united with the Son, and therefore just such love must be the being also of our human community with one another. We will be as different from one another as the Father is different from the Son, and just so we will be perfectly united to one another. Indeed, there will be nothing to any one of us but what she or he is from and for all the rest of us; we too will then be given perfect co-dependence. Our differences will be hierarchical. As ancient doctrine has it, each of us will embody the divine love for each other of us in the way and degree granted in this life— for me then to look up to Jonathan Edwards will not be occasion of envy but of pure joy in his achievement.

Since our communion with one another will be established by our inclusion in the differentiated communion of Father, Son, and Spirit, it will be determined also by the "processions" and "missions" that make that communion. The Father will

look on us as he looks on his Son: he will know who and what
he is as God by seeing what he has made of us. As the Son offers himself in obedience to the Father, the church will be both
the self, the "body," that he offers and participant in the act of
offering. And it is the very freedom of God as the Spirit that
will be our freedom in this fellowship. Such eschatological har-
dihood is now difficult for us, after so many bourgeois centuries. But again, if we are not up to it, this conference should
adjourn, for if the church has anything less grand to promise,
who needs it?

Fourth and last proposition. Let me recall the words of our
text: "The People of God, made one by sharing in the divine
unity, is...'a sacrament or sign and instrument of intimate union with God and of the unity of all humanity.'" It is the
church's sharing in the divine community that makes her a
community. And this is said by our fourth proposition not
only in the eschatological future tense but in the present tense
as well. Humanity's participation in the triune life is the final
goal of God's history; that was our text's third proposition.
But now we hear that *the church, in her communal unity, already*
anticipates humanity's life in the triune God. Therefore the shape
of the church's unity can reveal to all humanity its own fulfillment, its final unity with God and so with itself. Indeed, to be
thus the "sacrament" of humanity's godly destiny is the very
mission of the church.

I must begin with two negatives. First, that the church's
structure is grounded in and reveals God's triunity does not
mean that a mandatory church order can be derived from the
doctrine of Trinity: for example, I tried but could find no way
to deduce episcopal order from the Father's *monarchia*. Indeed,
one of the things that does follow from the church's participation in the triune life is the impossibility of such deductions.
For as the Spirit is the Son's freedom to act in historical responsibility, so is the Spouse of the Son thus freed. The church
might have turned down another path than the one that led to
the episcopate, and the choice was made in the church's own
communal responsibility.

But having said that, I must also say that this does not mean that the church can now reverse that decision, that the episcopate or similar chosen structures are not—in the old language of controversy—a matter of divine law. For the church's participation in the triune life means that the spirit that moves her historically is the Spirit that moves the Father and the Son, that the freedom in which the church makes her choices is God's own freedom. Thus if the episcopal order was indeed freely chosen by the church, that order is just *so* a matter of divine decision.

Second, the church's unity is established and only established by her participation in the perfect unity of the divine community. She must not, therefore, seek her unity in anything else; the structures of her community must be precisely the structures of her participation in God. As Protestant commissions for ecumenical dialogue are wont to insist, the church's structures must be transparent to God's initiative. This consideration leads directly to a list of positive and material prescriptions.

Prescription one. To say of actual structures of communal unity that they are to be utterly transparent to God's initiative is, of course, to say they are sacraments. For that is what a sacrament is, a structure of concrete communal unity that is transparent to God's action. Thus we have a fundamental rule for various projects, such as that of this conference: a right organizational chart of the church will have sacraments as its nodes. When we shape the church, what we are laying out in some pattern is sacraments and connections between sacraments.

It is a commonplace of current ecclesiology that the church's unity is fundamentally her unity at Eucharist, and that the other structures of her community must therefore be such as enable and delimit unity at Eucharist. The matter is perhaps more complex than that. But the so-called eucharistic ecclesiology is at least a good starting point for deliberations such as those of this conference.

Prescription two. The fulfillment of human community will be perfect love between wildly differentiated persons, because this community will be nothing but our participation in the love between the infinitely differentiated triune persons. The church is the anticipation of that final community, so let there be as many and as different roles in the life of the church as our ingenuity can discover. There is a traditional term for this character of the divine life: *perichoresis*, moving around and through one another—dancing with and around one another. The more of this in the church the better.

This is not a recommendation of general free enterprise, but rather the contrary, for we are talking about roles in unitary action. Father, Son, and Spirit, each in his role, do mutually always one action of God. Therefore whatever roles exist in the church must be roles in the doing of one thing, indeed in the doing of a same one thing that Father, Son, and Spirit mutually do. Or as Paul put it, churchly roles must have their sole *telos* in edifying the body of Christ.

What can never legitimately exist in the structure of the church is a role that finds its *telos* in a private or party agenda. Thus for random examples: an ordained priest can never be an entrepreneur, perhaps hanging out a shingle as a "pastoral counselor" or as some other sort of private practitioner, and the laws of the church must make it impossible for anyone even to try. A bishop in the exercise of his or her teaching office can have no personal opinions at all, and a right churchly structure will automatically silence him or her if this rule is broken. A bureau or agency can never become the turf or instrument of an ideological agenda, and a right churchly structure will provide stern oversight to prevent such a disaster.

Prescription three. In the political structure of the church, freedom as autonomy, as the possession of rights, is not a value. For in the triune community within which the church's community is enabled, Father, Son, and Spirit each subsists only from and for the others. The triune community and so the community of the church is a community only of glorious privileges, and of no rights at all.

So, for example, your speaker is a teaching theologian ordained within a particular church; this is a mighty privilege. On occasion, responsible hierarchs of that church have wanted to discipline my teaching. I have not liked this, but to have pretended to some sort of right to say what I please, even because I think it true, would have been to abandon my calling as a theologian. Paraphrasing a late very lamented: one should not belong to any church that could not excommunicate one. Or again, no one has a *right* to be a priest or bishop, any more than anyone has a *right* to be baptized into the church in the first place. Therefore, insofar as your church and mine began to ordain women because our culture regarded the church's previous practice as a violation of rights, we sinned grievously—and having said that, let me assure you of my conviction that women should indeed be priests and bishops.

Prescription four. A churchly differentiation of roles is hierarchical. The ideals of egalitarian democracy have nothing to say to the matter. For a central example: if our churchly order is such that we know where the *magisterium* lies, then in matters of teaching and mandated practice the word of those to whom that task has been given must outweigh the word of a thousand academic theologians or other laity who think they do not agree. Or again, it is not merely concern for good order that dictates that some preside at Eucharist and some receive at Eucharist, and that this order is not reversible. Yet again, it is not only to promote church growth that evangelism must be a task of those who receive Eucharist and not of those who preside.

Prescription five. We can dare to live such organic community, we can defy our own and others' fears about "authoritarianism" and so forth, because and only because the communal spirit that moves the church's several roles and orchestrates their symphony is God's own Spirit. Did we not believe that the Spirit guides the church through history, every ancient lamentation about hierarchy would have to be taken as obviously veridical. It is immediately plain: no churchly arrangements—episcopal or congregational, papal or individualist— can in their own entity as historical institutions preserve the church from tyranny, apostasy, or any other of the evils that afflict religious communities. Indeed, faith that the church can so much as claim to be now the church is always faith that God uses and has used the church's structures of historical community to keep this created community within the divine community. This is to say that all proper churchly roles are *charisms* in the New Testament's precise sense. In the New Testament we see first charisms that are unpredictable and ritually and officially unspecifiable; then we see charisms granted by a rite and constituting official functions. The order of the church must encompass and be upheld by charisms of both sorts. And with respect to the second, our chief concern must be that they are so inserted into the whole pattern of the church that they indeed are and remain charisms.

Prescription six. The church participates in the divine life as she is one with the Son, and so dances with the Son around and in the Father and the Spirit; and yet of course she is also other than the Son, and so within the triune life dances with the Father and the Spirit around and in the Son. In the language of the New Testament, she is at once the Body and the Spouse of the Son. Since her own community is nothing but this participation, these relations too must be "effectively signified" in her. I am about to utter some commonplaces of ecumenical theology, but where better to utter them than where a denomination is considering its future shape? For reasons already noted, we may center our analyses on the Eucharist.

The sacramental structure of the church must on the one hand display that the church and Lord are over against each other, that between them there is meeting. At the Eucharist, this is accomplished by the fact that those who minister and those who receive Christ's presence are not the same. As the classic formula has it, the bishop or presbyter appears at eucharist *in persona Christi*. Yet the celebrant does not so appear in his or her own right; on the contrary, the gathered congregation is the fountain and freedom of the celebrant's role, as the Father and the Spirit are of the Son.

Yet this meeting is accomplished within the unity of the Son with his own Body. And so, as many ecumenical agreements say, the congregation is precisely by receiving Christ's presence swept up into the Son's eternal offering of himself to the Father, and into the Son's possession and sending of the Spirit into the world. This is displayed at eucharist in that the bishop or other pastor, who represents Christ to the assembly, simultaneously leads the assembly in prayer and sacrifice to the Father and in unified invocation of the Spirit, of the congregation's own mission in the world.

Prescription seven. It will be seen that both as Christ's representative to the people and as the leader of the body of Christ in Christ's relation to the Father and the Son, the eucharistic celebrant has the unity of the congregation as his or her task. Here is the last ecumenical platitude: those ordained to be eucharistic celebrants, at whatever level or connection of the church, are first of all ministers of unity. Their charism is the charism of the shepherd, who keeps the flock determinate and together.

Abstractly, there are various ways in which this ministry could itself be structured and in which other roles could so be related to it as themselves to serve the unity it serves. In actual history—which, we remember, is in the hands of the Spirit—it is the structure of metropolitan bishops as ministers of unity among what we now call "congregations," and of patriarchs as ministers of unity among the bishops, and of a primatial ministry of the one church, that has done this.

The case of the Lutherans in this respect is merely chaotic and lamentable. But it seems to me that the Anglican communion's position over against the rest of the church is also somewhat odd, so long as the only patriarch in view is the English sovereign. I have heard that the central structure of the Episcopal Church is on the agenda which many of you have brought to this conference. As you consider the matter, perhaps you might well keep the ancient structures in mind.

As triune, God is community in himself. His destiny for humankind is to take us into that community. The church anticipated this destiny, and so can reveal it. The structures of the church must do this.

J. Stephen Freeman

The Church, Structure, and Reform

THERE IS A DESIRE for change in the Episcopal Church. Though there is very little consensus among us about what changes are needed, a sense is growing within the church that things cannot continue as they are. Theological debates defy resolution; membership statistics remain less than encouraging; financial needs continue to outstrip resources. Something is wrong that goes beyond any of the current "hot-button" issues, something that can only be addressed by fundamental, structural change.[1] That desire for change goes beyond a dissatisfaction with the chaos, costliness, and ineffectiveness of the national church bureaucracy, and includes both the diocesan and local church levels.

As Stanley Hauerwas and William Willimon point out in *Resident Aliens*, the disillusionment and frustration on the part of clergy and people toward the various institutions of the church have become a common element in the culture of the mainline churches. Church members have no particular "brand loyalty": an increasing number of laypersons switch denominations as easily as they change grocery stores. Often they have no regard whatsoever for the institutional structures that extend beyond the local congregation, and many have no sense of why they should. Clergy burnout is sometimes described as epidemic, itself a reflection of fundamental problems within the immediate culture of the local parish. Hauerwas and Willimon note that many contemporary pastors use words such as "abuse," "seduction," and "prostitution" when they speak of their feelings about their roles as pastors.

Pastors come to despise what they are and to hate the community that made them that way. Because the church is not a
place to worship God, but rather a therapeutic center for the
meeting of one another's unchecked, unexamined needs, the
pastor is exhausted.[2]

They credit these pastoral problems to a church structured for
consumerism. Careful reflection both on the current state of
the church and the role played by the various structures that
comprise it is long overdue. This paper is offered as part of the
process of that reflection.

There are several questions which deserve particular attention. The first is the very nature of the church. What consti-
tutes the church? That is, what is truly essential in the life of
the church and what is merely beneficial? To answer this is to
know what we *cannot* change and what we *can*. The second
area for our attention is the relationship of structure to this essential part of the church's life. Do our present parish, diocesan, and national structures enhance and encourage this
essential life, or do they distract and distort? If they do harm,
how might they be changed to help? Finally, what should be
the primary concerns informing any proposal for structural reform? What does the church of the next century, in this culture, need to look like in order to be faithful to the gospel of
Jesus Christ?

The Church as Eucharistic Community

The reformers of the sixteenth century came to the conclusion that the church's essential nature is to be found in its existence as a worshiping community. In Article XIX of the
Articles of Religion, they defined the church as the place where
the "pure Word of God is preached and the Sacraments duly
ministered according to Christ's ordinance." Every other action
of the church could, in theory, be carried out by something
wholly apart from God or the gospel of Christ. The one activity that uniquely reveals us to be the church is our worship. Indeed, the consensus on this understanding has become so

universal that it is a commonplace in ecumenical circles to define the church as a "eucharistic community."[3]

To describe the church's essential nature as a eucharistic or worshiping community is not to limit church to some few hours of weekly gathering. Rather, the whole of the church's life, within and without its formal liturgy, is to be seen and defined by the Eucharist. By presenting to God "our selves, our souls and bodies," we gather the whole of our life into the offering of bread and wine. In the liturgy we not only ask the Holy Spirit to sanctify our offering of bread and wine, we ask that *we* be sanctified as well. The Eucharist is the church offered to God and by God to the world. This is our essential life together.

As a eucharistic community, the church is the creation of the Holy Spirit. It is not an institution to which the Holy Spirit is later added, or which calls the Holy Spirit to its aid when it celebrates sacraments. The Spirit is not the possession of the church, dispensed by its ordained clergy to its people. The church itself is the creation of the Holy Spirit.[4] The church is thus not a sacred trust given to one generation to be handed on to the next, or a human institution to be carefully guarded or even carefully reformed for human purposes. The church today, as much as the church at Pentecost, is constituted by and utterly dependent upon the Holy Spirit. As such, the church cannot be institutionalized, for "where the Spirit of the Lord is, there is freedom" (2 Cor. 3:17). An institutionalized vision of the Spirit would be an inherently flawed vision of the church.

As the creation of the Holy Spirit, the church is catholic; that is, wherever it exists, it exists as a whole (*katholikos*) church.[5] It is incorrect to speak of "branches" of the church, or even of this "part" of the church. Wherever the church gathers, it is the church. The local eucharistic community is no more a mere "part" of the body of Christ, the local franchise of the universal body, than the eucharistic bread and wine on the altar is a "part" of the body or blood of Christ. The church is one and catholic. Christ is not divided (1 Cor. 1:13). The local church gains its existence and authority from the Holy Spirit and not from its participation in deliberative bodies or organizations at a distance removed from the eucharistic community. Its unity with other local communities is also a gift of the Holy Spirit. The church is one, because it is always the same church which the Holy Spirit creates. This unity, in the Episcopal Church, is manifested in the ministry of bishop and in the fullness of eucharistic fellowship.

The church as eucharistic community does not exist in the abstract. Theories of an "invisible church" inevitably do an injustice to the concrete reality of the body of Christ. As a concrete eucharistic community, the church has concrete needs: it needs to meet in a specific place, and may well own property; it needs to have a visible and identifiable ministry in continuity with the historic succession. The church has a need for identifiable institutions, but such institutions exist *only by permission and not by necessity*—that is, for the church's benefit— and do not and cannot *constitute* the church.

In its concrete existence the church is manifest primarily as a local eucharistic community. Thus, the church consists of real people in a real place who actually share eucharist together. This is not to deny the reality of church beyond local boundaries, but to locate the *essential nature* of the church in the local eucharistic community. Structures such as General Conventions, executive councils, or diocesan offices may be useful to the life of the church, but they are not the church. The church could and has had different structures for governance and program. The present configuration of the Episcopal Church has its shape primarily for the church's benefit. If the benefit comes to be insufficient, then structures should be changed.

Understanding the church as a eucharistic community helps us to see what is truly essential for the life of the church. It helps us to understand why it is that the church often does quite well in times of great persecution when all of the normal support structures that so dominate our attention are swept away. The house churches of China as well as the struggling yet faithful churches of Eastern Europe and Russia demonstrate that the church is dependent upon the Spirit for its existence and not upon the supporting structures we erect. Indeed, in both China and Russia, the local eucharistic community frequently has had to exist *in spite* of its official structures. The loss of property, committees, bylaws, and vestries (or their equivalents), the outlawing of church offices, official charities, and benevolent societies have all been the lot of the church in any number of places in this century (places where, it should be noted, the church has prospered and made manifest the gospel in all its power).

The Structures of the Eucharistic Community

The church understood as a eucharistic community provides a rule by which we can measure the service rendered by a given structure, or a lens through which we may view the proper relationship of structures to the life of the church. I want to direct our attention, at this point, to an examination of those structures.

As noted above, the fact that the church does not exist as an abstract concept but as a local reality necessitates that there be certain structures. Who distributes the church's alms, who provides the bread and wine, who educates and trains its clergy, who baptizes and catechizes its people are questions that require some structure to their answer. It will be this person and not that, this group and not that, and they will all have relationships one to another which will inevitably constitute some form of structure. *How* they are structured, however, must be consonant with the essential nature of the church. There is always the danger that the nonessential structures that exist to benefit the church will in fact impede and inhibit the church's true life. The often sad story of church history could furnish any number of examples.

The role that structures have played in the life of the church has not always been the same. A revolution in human thinking emerged in the sixteenth and seventeenth centuries, giving rise to our modern period. That revolution changed how we view ourselves, our world, and our place within that world, including the purpose and function of the structures we create. It was not the first such revolution, but it is the one that has most affected us. It has had a particular impact on the shape and function of the structures in the church. This is important to understand, particularly when the language we use to describe many of our structures often remains the same long after those structures have become something else entirely. For example, the ministerial role which we call "bishop" long ago ceased to resemble its original model. Bishops in the first few centuries of the church served a community called a *parochia* (today's modern "parish"), while a "diocese" referred to what we today would think of as a province. Bishops were more rectors than directors of large, geographically expansive organizations.

The revolution in ideas that ushered in and created the modern period have a number of striking features, several of which tend to dominate the present structural life of the church. Charles Taylor, for years the Chichele Professor of Moral Philosophy at Oxford, has described the development of the modern consciousness and its effect on our world. He notes the shift from a more communal understanding of human existence to the radical individualism of the modern age as among the most important of the changes. Along with this change in our self-image has come a dominant position for the role of the will. We have come to see ourselves as individuals who see and understand, who choose and make decisions. We relate and belong to one another only in the most voluntary ways. Taylor writes that the medieval catholic had been

> a passenger in the ecclesial ship on its journey to God. But for Protestantism, there can be no passengers. This is because there is no ship in the Catholic sense, no common movement carrying humans to salvation. Each believer rows his or her own boat.[6]

Our theology and piety have come to champion individual experience and the importance of personal responsibility. We have come to be consumers of religious faith. We have become the kind of people for whom the widest possible application of the scientific method seems obvious. We organize for tasks, make goals, plans, implement, and evaluate. This "objective" application of organizational science has produced wealth and technology beyond anything earlier generations might have dreamed. It has also reached certain limitations that are only becoming apparent in our own century. The dominance of intellect and will, the vision of the human as individual, as producer and consumer, has clearly brought benefits. It has produced democracy, capitalism, and tremendous wealth. However, it lacks the resources for balancing freedom with the requirements of community; for creating a public moral discourse capable of sustaining virtue; of establishing acceptable criteria for saying "no" to the unlimited demands of the will.

This shift has also brought about changes in the structural life of the church. An inherently conservative organization, the church frequently lags behind the surrounding culture in adopting more popular world-views. The modern church was slow to take up the structural models created by this new understanding of the human. The American church brought with it, with some modification, the structures of the European church, themselves the product of an earlier Christendom. Those structures presumed a static world in which society was already converted. The church's structures paralleled those of government, with the assumption that as the government looked after the temporal world, so the church would look after the spiritual. America's success as the world's first secular power gave added weight to the metaphor of "practicality" engendered by the Enlightenment's revolutionary view of the human. The rapid expanse of America, with its political and material success, provided a strong incentive for the church to change the nature of its structures.

For the Episcopal Church that change took place in and around 1919. Interestingly, the same change was brought about in other mainline denominations around the same time.[7] Ostensibly, those changes were to bring the know-how of American industry to bear on the social ills of society and the great challenge of the missionary endeavor. The result was neither. Instead, the church came to see the task of ministry in an essentially secularized fashion. Today the church commissions studies, analyzes data, formulates goals, establishes commit-tees, creates budgets, implements programs, and evaluates re-sults (sometimes). The church has become a place in which the idea of a "decade of evangelism," complete with the necessary supporting structures, seems a good idea. It is important to note that there is no record of planning meetings in the early church, no hint of goals (at least not in our sense of the word), nor even of committees or budgets. My point here is not just that such structures did not exist, but that it would never have occurred to the saints of the early church to have had such structures.[8] It is equally important for us to note (since our modern world-view is particularly impressed with measurable results) that the absence of the kind of structures that domi-nate the modern church seems to have impeded the growth and spread of the early church in no way whatsoever.

The present crisis, however, is the need for judging the faith-fulness of our structures to the gospel of Jesus Christ and the church's role in the world. Do our corporate structures serve or impede the gospel? Do they obscure or reveal the church as a eucharistic community, dependent upon the Spirit? It is my contention that the corporate model not only impedes the gos-pel in our present context, but runs the risk of leading the Episcopal Church down the same road of decay and diminu-tion as has largely visited the churches of Europe, if for differ-ent reasons. That contention is rooted in the observation that our structures necessarily focus on the church as institution, that is, as an entity configured in a manner analogous to a business or corporation with religious purpose. That same vi-sion blinds us to the essential nature of the church and the character and practices required of our members necessary to sustain the church as a eucharistic community dependent upon the Spirit. We have structured ourselves for spiritual failure.

The structures of the national church are the easiest to de-tail in this vein. The office of Presiding Bishop as a ministry devoid of direct responsibility for a eucharistic community, as well as the Executive Council and the bureaucracy which has grown up in support of these structures, are the creatures of the General Convention of 1919, specifically created to copy the corporate structures of industrial America.[9] The language that accompanied that creation makes it clear that the church uncritically adopted the corporate culture along with its assumptions about the world and its response to human activity. Those assumptions are today themselves the subject of evaluation even within the corporate world. Those assumptions also traveled far beyond the confines of the national church. Local dioceses, as well as many parishes, have increasingly adopted corporate models of management and self-understanding, eventually incurring a stagnant or declining pattern of membership as well as an unsustainable financial burden.

It is worth noting that the creation of the national church bureaucracy was directly fueled by expansionist visions within American foreign policy. Following the Spanish-American War, the Episcopal Church began its first missions to Central and South America, arguing for a "Christianization of the Monroe Doctrine."[10] The impetus of foreign missions and central coordination of social outreach gave rise to the creation of the central bureaucracy of 1919. Although both foreign mission and social ministry are gospel activities, the rhetoric surrounding those lofty national goals (and thus presumably the goals themselves) was dominated by the secular vision of the culture at large. The church championed the new vision of America as the fount of democracy and solver of social ills and sought to establish itself in a parallel structure providing "national leadership." Whether in the growth of Protestantism in Latin America to provide a safe context for democracy or in the later promotion of Christian mission as a bulwark against communism, the "national ideal" which built and expanded the national church concept consistently paralleled whatever vision was dominating American culture at the time. The vision of that culture has continually changed, but the mechanisms of cultural domination within the structures of the church continue. At present, foreign missions have all but ceased to be a part of the national church's work. However, the issues of race, gender, and sexuality dominate the national church's attention in a manner and in terms indistinguishable from those of the culture at large.

The church today is better situated to evaluate the validity of the cultural world-view that shaped the General Convention of 1919 and the structures it created. That world-view presupposed that the environment in which we live and work is knowable, predictable, and subject to control and manipulation. The period had great hopes for the solution of human misery through the wide application of the scientific method and the rise of the social sciences. Social programs and intervention, properly designed and implemented, were thought of as a panacea to the ills of the nation. Although we have learned much and benefited much from such assumptions, we have also learned their limitations. Much of our world is beyond our knowing, its complexity beyond the ability to control or predict. Human beings do not flourish in command economies, nor are they subject to planning or engineering. Corporations are rushing to remove the regimentation of bureaucratic structures and nurture the spontaneity and creativity of smaller groups of persons. Governments are reexamining their own efforts of social engineering and control as many of the problems they sought to solve have proven intractable.

From a gospel perspective, the world-view of 1919 now seems inexcusably bound by human pride. Jesus taught his disciples that the Spirit "blows where it chooses," adding, "You do not know where it comes from or where it goes" (John 3:8). How could we have planned and organized for the future of a church which is dependent upon the Spirit? Christ had told us that the "kingdom is not coming with things that can be observed" (Luke 17:20), and yet we established a pattern within our structures that professionalized our ministries, erecting a career ladder that rewarded "success" and punished "failure" with money and responsibility, and did so with a set of criteria not easily distinguished from those of the business community.

The message of a church that structured itself after the fashion of the corporate and industrial world was an implicit blessing on the nature and character of those structures. The church became a corporate structure surrounded by corporate structures, a player on a level field. Its argument with the world became fixed on the setting of goals. With proper values, the industrial world could be the agent of God's kingdom. This attitude has given birth to a host of petty resolutions in General Convention in which the church addresses such issues as the American banking system, offering critiques that amount to little more than "fine tuning," or arguments about management policy. At the same time, the existence of the church became questionable. If a well-intentioned industrial world can do the job, who needs a church? This offers one explanation for recent efforts by many local churches to reposition themselves in the "market." Churches are now beginning to specialize in spirituality. Unfortunately, in our pluralistic culture, that niche, too, has formidable competition.

Structure as the Servant of the Church's Character

Jesus' establishment of his community presumed from the beginning that the church differed from the world not only in its *message*, but also in the *nature* and *character* of its life. In describing the leadership of the church, Jesus contrasted it with the style of the Gentiles, who "lord it over them" (Matt. 20:25). The character and practices necessary to sustain the community of Jesus were never those of the surrounding culture. Humility, meekness, the renunciation of violence and coercion were required of his eucharistic fellowship. St. Paul can note that among the Corinthians "not many of you were wise by human standards, not many were powerful, not many were of noble birth" (1 Cor. 1:26). Instead, he says, God "chose what is foolish in the world to shame the wise" (v. 27). The eucharistic community of Jesus, by its very character and practices, proclaims the gospel to the world and judges the wisdom of the world. God chose the "things that are not, to reduce to nothing things that are" (v. 28).

By endorsing the structures of the industrial world, the modern church acknowledges that talent and wisdom, noble birth and good skills will triumph over the weakness of the poor. The marginalized will remain on the margins. Losers will remain lost and without position within a managerial structure that rewards the skillful use of power. The church may champion the cause of the poor and marginalized in its rhetoric and pronouncements, but its structures will inherently restrict their deliverance within the church as much as within the world. The church's occasional advocacy for the poor is most often indistinguishable from that of the state. In both cases it is the rich and powerful speaking *for* the poor. In neither case is it the exaltation of the "humble and meek," nor the rich and powerful becoming poor and weak for the sake of the world.

What are the practices necessary to sustain the community of Jesus in our present world? What should be the character of our structures in light of the gospel? The gospel assumes that the most difficult task facing a Christian is being a faithful member of the eucharistic community, because being part of such a community requires the acceptance of the Christian story as definitive for life and the virtues. It requires the difficult practice of agapaic love, where weakness is exalted over strength and forgiveness displaces vengeance. It requires that Christians live in such a way that if Christ's kingdom does not come, their life and actions will have been absurd. The professionalization of the Christian church constantly threatens to substitute a religiously-oriented institution for this dynamic presence of Christ's body.

The structures that should characterize the church in today's culture look far different in the main from those at present. There are several areas to which I would like to draw particular attention. These are: structures of hospitality (how do we welcome?); structures for catechesis (how do we educate?); structures for the preparation of the ordained ministry; structures for fellowship and discipline between local communities; and structures of governance. All of these activities are necessitated by the eucharistic nature of the church and should be formed in keeping with that character.

A eucharistic community dependent upon the Spirit will necessarily be structured for hospitality. The disenfranchised and marginalized, children and strangers must be not only *welcomed* but *honored* by the community of Jesus. In the church understood as eucharistic community, the weakest members are as *necessary* as the strongest and most talented. They are more than objects for ministry: they constitute the church. Stanley Hauerwas has said of this:

> The Christian community's openness to new life and our conviction of the sovereignty of God over that life are but two sides of the same conviction. Christians believe that we have the time in this existence to care for new life, especially as such life is dependent and vulnerable, because it is not our task to rule this world or to "make our mark on history." We can thus take the time to live in history as God's people who have nothing more important to do than to have and care for children. For it is the Christian claim that knowledge and love of God is fostered by service to the neighbor, especially the most helpless, as in fact that is where we find the kind of Kingdom our God would have us serve.[11]

In structuring itself for hospitality the church must ask itself what or whom it exists to serve. If we have "nothing more important to do than to have and care for children," why are children frequently relegated to a "tolerated" role in the life of the church? What barriers are created by vocabulary and literacy requirements of the liturgy? Episcopalians are largely unaware of the stumbling block presented by the ethnic (English) exclusivity of our language and customs. A careful examination of the church with these questions in mind would likely reveal the fact that we are frequently structured in such a way to preserve a particular socio-economic and ethnic culture rather than welcome the weakest of society.

A second necessary structure would be one constructed for catechesis. If the church is to differ from the culture in the manner of its life as well as its message, then strong catechesis is presupposed. Faithful members must know and accept the Christian narrative as normative for their lives. Attention to the formation of character and the cultivation of practices that can sustain Christians in the face of a hostile environment will require intentional catechesis that goes far beyond most current models of Christian education. The church's current domination by the structures of the corporate world illustrate the dangers of a membership which has not been properly or thoroughly catechized. The Christian gospel requires that we renounce the "powers of this world" and the ethos which nurtures them. A church without such a converted understanding will likely replicate the world within its own structures, thus rendering the gospel of no effect.[12]

Structures for the preparation of ordained ministry also should change. Current structures tend to be dominated by institutions oriented toward the academy, only marginally responsible to the eucharistic communities whose leaders they train. Scholars are useful to the church, but may be the wrong persons for training priests and deacons. Ordained ministry, as a *practice*, is learned best by imitation rather than by the mere exchange of information.[13] Seminaries may even be the wrong venue for such discipleship to take place. Apprenticeship might be the far better route. The current process toward ordination which is largely carried out by strangers who read a few papers and conduct relatively brief interviews seems strangely remote from the intimate knowledge and careful expectations needed for those ordained to serve in the eucharistic community. Some of this remoteness is the natural outcome of the distance between authority structures and the communities which they serve.

Equally important in our structures for training ordained ministry is the unconscious tendency of our system to educate primarily for acceptance within an educational and socio-economic class. The Episcopal Church remains a predominately white, middle- and upper-class church because it refuses to adapt to the legitimate indigenous needs of other cultural groups within our society. Although some attention has been paid to recognized minorities, other groups have been excluded almost intentionally. The most striking example of this is blue-collar and poor white America. The rapid growth of fundamentalist and Pentecostal churches within this group stems primarily from their ability and willingness to ordain clergy who are indigenous to that group. Anglican discomfort with the "bad taste" of the groups that make up the underclass of America (though economically now entering "middle America") have dogged the church's mission efforts at least since the time of the Wesleys. The demand for an "educated" ordained ministry should be balanced against the needs of a culture in which education can be synonymous with class. The Anglican churches of Africa have successfully overcome this problem and provide models for the establishment of indigenous ministries.

Structures for fellowship and discipline are also necessitated by the church as eucharistic community. Without communion between eucharistic communities the church ceases to be catholic. The wholeness or fullness granted by the Spirit is manifested in the community's refusal to be merely local. Local distinctions (race, ethnicity, gender, social status) are overcome because the Spirit baptizes all into the one body. There is no distinction. The ancient structure which preserves this communion is centered in the bishop. Communion between bishops is and should be an outward sign of the true unity of the church, a manifestation that the church in one place is the same church found in another.

Eucharistic discipline is necessarily part of this same structure. Failure to exercise discipline within the eucharistic church is as serious a danger to the church's catholicity as failure to maintain fellowship. Institutional unity enforced through the property laws of the state is a poor substitute for the biblical and early church model of eucharistic unity. Although Episcopalians apparently find the ancient discipline of excommunication between and among bishops or within a congregation to be repulsive, it is much to be preferred to the current canonical procedures of trial and deposition (in the case of errant clergy) or of trial and legal confiscation of property (in the case of errant or protesting congregations). The current model relies on a use of coercive state-sponsored violence (removal from office or property) nowhere condoned in the Scriptures and hardly in keeping with gospel injunctions. The cessation of eucharistic fellowship allows for greater possibility of renewed and repentant relationships without resorting to coercion. Structures that depend upon the state for their success are structures of violence, inconsonant with the teachings of Christ. The fear of lowering the legal bonds that hold the church together as institution needs to be examined in the light of the gospel. What kind of community is it which has to be held together by such a use of coercive law?

Careful attention should be given to every structure of the church that is distanced from the local eucharistic community. In a culture which is dominated by the world of corporate management, such structures will almost inevitably adopt such a model, betraying the unique mission and nature of the church. The national bureaucracy created in 1919 should be dismantled as an unnecessary structure inherently removed from the embodied eucharistic life of the church. The office of Presiding Bishop, divorced from the eucharistic community of the church since 1919, should be returned to a post held by a sitting diocesan bishop, or at least given some form of eucharistic jurisdiction.

The problems created by our model of diocese and parish deserve careful attention as well. Most dioceses throughout the Anglican and Catholic world have bishops whose ministry is largely divorced from the local eucharistic communities of which they are the stated heads. The ministry of bishop has become inherently administrative and bureaucratic rather than pastoral and eucharistic. When bishops come to function like absentee landlords, the local eucharistic community ceases to have episcopal ministry in anything other than a ceremonial fashion. This can be contrasted to the effectiveness of missionary bishops, the few remaining examples of non-administrative bishops sprinkled across the pages of later church history. Augustine of Canterbury, Patrick of Ireland, or Jackson Kemper in the United States demonstrate the tremendous possibilities when the ministry of bishop is returned to its eucharistic roots. It is worth noting that most of our dioceses reach a certain size, manageable by an administrative structure incorporating a single bishop, or one with an assisting bishop. At such a point dioceses tend to become stable and relatively static. Some version of Parkinson's Law ("work expands to fill the time available for its completion") seems to be applicable, with the corollary that until we change our structures, we will not grow. The genius of the small group movement in church

growth circles lies precisely in its insight that structure and
growth are directly related.

General Convention, a structure which parallels the ancient
synods of the church, is an entirely different matter. As earlier
stated, it is necessary for local communities to come together
in common or they become merely local and cease to be catholic. However, local eucharistic communities are not mere representatives of the greater whole. A local community, created by
the Holy Spirit, is the catholic (whole) church. At present,
General Convention acts as a board of directors (a role played
by Executive Council between Conventions). In such a role,
the temptation to create parallel, permanent structures to embody a "national" church seems to have been irresistible. General Convention's preferred role should be that of council or
synod. Convention should carefully avoid usurping the proper
function of more local synods or of the local eucharistic communities themselves. One means of reforming toward this end
would be to remove General Convention from the calendar (it
now meets every three years by canon law), and make it a true
convocation—that is, a council that is called into existence by
the local communities. This could be done by revising the canons to require that a certain number or proportion of dioceses
vote to request a General Convention. Added to this should be
a stipulation that the purpose of the General Convention be
specifically stated in the call. Such reforms would move the
Convention in the direction of serving the church rather than
defining or governing the church. A council is a necessary
economy, useful for the well-being of the church. However, our
current constitutional arrangement comes dangerously close to
establishing General Convention as the true and ultimate form of
the church in which other, more local forms merely participate.

Local synods such as diocesan meetings and provincial synods should be preferred to national gatherings in an effort to
avoid the creation of bureaucratic structures which abstract
the church's mission and ministry away from the context of
the eucharistic community. Even here, there is a need for vigi-
lance lest we create multiple local forms of our present system.[14] Philip Turner has noted that councils, conventions, and

synods are frequently poor forums for the address of moral issues. The question of who is speaking and to whom, as well as the poor theological grounding and formulation of the resolutions usually produced by such gatherings, are among the concerns he cites.[15]

I would take Turner's observations a step further. The gospel *cannot* be proclaimed in the form of resolution and pronouncement if that resolution or pronouncement exists abstracted from the actual life of the church. Resolutions or declarations of the church should be nothing more than the verbal expressions of the character of the Christian community. Anything less will be rightly heard as hypocrisy. Council and synod should not speak as one voice among others, trading the church's opinion with the opinions of other organizations or corporations. General Convention in 1991 approved over five hundred resolutions in ten days on subjects ranging from the American banking system to human sexuality. Such cavalier treatment of the gospel makes a mockery of the church's role as teacher.

The gospel is an enfleshed reality, the tabernacling of God among humanity. The church as eucharistic community *is* the gospel of Jesus Christ. The questions addressed by resolutions are appropriately addressed to the church and ask of the church, "How should we order our lives if this is the truth?" It is highly questionable whether the church should seek to control the outcome of history through its legislative actions. The temptation to endorse the violence of the state when it suits the church's perceived ends has typically been irresistible. In contrast, the gospel seems to present the church as the *outcome* of the coming of the kingdom rather than the agent of its arrival. The primary concern of the church should be to live in a manner which is faithful to the character of Jesus. To accept responsibility for history runs dangerously close to idolatry.[16]

The Church and the Structures of the World

Prior to concluding, I feel some need to digress for a moment to address an obvious question raised by the approach which I have been advocating. In *The Crisis in Moral Teaching in the Episcopal Church,* Allan Parrent and Philip Turner make use of Ernst Troeltsch's classic church-versus-sect distinction to describe the church's relationship to the surrounding culture. The "church-type" ecclesiology seeks to describe the position of the church which sees itself as a partner with the state and other official forces, sharing in the responsibility for the "moral ethos" and the "civic virtues and public morality" of a culture. The "sect-type" ecclesiology describes the position held by those churches which define themselves primarily as "over-and-against" a culture, or as primarily defining themselves by faithfulness to gospel command rather than by impact or role in society. The church-type ecclesiology is best exemplified by state churches, the sect-type by the primitive church or later Anabaptist and free-church traditions. Parrent argues that Anglicanism has traditionally held to the church-type position and that it needs to reassert itself strongly in that model. He cites the alarms of theologians such as Richard John Neuhaus in his call to reclaim the Anglican church-type position. He fears the unraveling of American society without the church's moral leadership, yet he fails to see how far the culture has moved from such management strategies. Turner apparently sympathizes with this view, with reservations which move in a more sectarian direction.[17]

This paper has argued strongly for what may be characterized as a sectarian approach for the Episcopal Church, and may too easily be criticized or dismissed on that account. Although I must agree that Anglicanism has traditionally held to a church-type ecclesiology in its relationship with society, it must be granted that this historical fact does not necessarily establish this pattern as God's will for Anglicans. Our identification with the state, or with the social order, cannot be shown to have delivered its promised impact on the moral ethos of society. Slavery was addressed primarily by sectarian evangelicals; war has never been adequately addressed by those espousing a church-type ecclesiology; the current discussions of moral issues by the churches reflect nothing more than the confusion and pluralism of the culture at large. Their impact is negligible, if any.

The church-type approach to society assumes for the church a stewardship of history and a share in the responsibility for the outcomes of history. Yet the gospel of Christ bears witness to the world that God alone is Lord of history. The refusal to take up utilitarian approaches to the world (the essential mode for the modern church), is to bear witness not only to the moral judgments of Christ, but to God's means for bringing those judgments about. Caesar will always resort to violence as his final means for achieving his goals of limited justice. Acceptance of that violence has always meant a fundamental compromise of the gospel. In baptism, we renounce the "evil powers of this world which corrupt and destroy the creatures of God." In New Testament terms, such language always included the principalities and powers that constitute the state.

Allan Parrent's call for Anglicans to reclaim their church-type position with regard to society represents a nostalgic longing for a Christendom which has ceased to exist.[18] The church-type ecclesiology is the product of a relationship which presupposes the majority status of the church (as in Constantine's empire or Reformation England). It is a comical position to be held by a shrinking denomination of less than one percent of a nation, in a culture which is increasingly pluralistic and which explicitly repudiates any organic relationship between the state and religious groups. The Episcopal Church must now reexamine its sectarian position whether it wants to or not. I am arguing in this paper that this reexamination is both welcome and proper.

The Episcopal Church, like many of the denominations around us, stands in a place of crisis today, a time in which directions can be changed and fundamental reassessments can take place. More than the political realities of the world have changed in the last few years. The culture in which the church lives has taken on a new cast. We are no longer in Christendom, and no longer enjoy a privileged position. The erosion of central authorities in nation and culture threaten our world with new forms of chaos and the violence of unchecked anarchies. The church as presently configured is unsuited to the gospel ministry in the world ahead of us. There is an urgency to our need for structural reform. The church needs to be structured for the formation of gospel ministry. The world increasingly needs a church that discernably embodies the gospel. We do not know what the future holds, except that God has promised to meet us constantly at that point. The task before the church is to leave behind the structures of an age that has disappeared and embrace the structures which prepare us to meet the age to come, an age which is not of this world nor yet glimpsed by those who are in the world.

Endnotes

1. For background on the call for structural reform see my article, "Structural Reform Needed," in *The Living Church* (June 7, 1992), pp. 11-12.

2. Stanley Hauerwas and William Willimon, *Resident Aliens* (Nashville: Abingdon, 1989), pp. 123-124.

3. One of the fullest treatments of the subject is John Zizioulas's *Being as Communion: Studies in Personhood and the Church* (Crestwood, N.Y.: St. Vladimir's Press, 1985), particularly pp. 123-260.

4. Colin Gunton has written most persuasively of the need for locating ecclesiology within a pneumatological rather than a christological setting. See his *The Promise of Trinitarian Theology* (Edinburgh: T&T Clark, 1991), pp. 58-83.

5. Section VI of the Moscow Agreed Statement between Anglicans and Orthodox (*Anglican-Orthodox Dialogue*) says, "In each local eucharistic celebration the visible unity and catholicity of the church is manifested fully" (Crestwood, N.Y.: St. Vladimir's Press, 1985), p. 56.

6. Charles Taylor, *Sources of the Self: The Making of the Modern Identity* (Cambridge: Harvard University Press, 1989), p. 217.

7. Craig Dykstra and James Hudnut-Beumler's "The National Organizational Structures of Protestant Denominations: An Invitation to a Conversation" in *The Organizational Revolution* (Louisville: John Knox/Westminster, 1992), pp. 306-330, provides an excellent overview of the corporate mentality that shaped denominational management over the course of the century. Of equal interest is Louis B. Weeks's essay, "The Incorporation of the Presbyterians," in the same volume (pp. 37-54).

8. As will be discussed at a later point, one reason such structures would never have occurred to the pre-Constantinian church is that it had not taken co-responsibility for the culture and the outcome of history along with the

state. The shift that occurs in the fourth century pushes the church toward the *necessity* of sharing in the *anxiety* of the Caesars, who must seek to control and force history to come to a conclusion favorable to the empire.

9. Articles appearing in contemporary journals and news pieces support this observation. Of particular interest are a series of interviews with deputies appearing in the November 15, 1919 issue of *The Churchman*.

10. Quoted by Ian T. Douglas in "'A Light to the Nations': Episcopal Foreign Missions in Historical Perspective" *Anglican and Episcopal History* 41:4, p. 457. I am deeply indebted to Douglas's article for the points offered in this paragraph. The quotations he includes are particularly enlightening.

11. Stanley Hauerwas, *A Community of Character: Toward a Constructive Christian Social Ethic* (Notre Dame: University of Notre Dame Press, 1981), p. 226.

12. John Westerhoff and Stanley Hauerwas' *Schooling Christians: Holy Experiments in American Education* (Grand Rapids: Eerdmans, 1992) provides an excellent collection of essays on the larger question of the education of Christians in the face of an increasingly indifferent or hostile culture.

13. I am using the term "practice" in the sense defined by Alasdair MacIntyre in his *After Virtue: A Study in Moral Theology* (Notre Dame: Notre Dame University Press, 1984). See particularly pp. 181-203.

14. The principle of subsidiarity, first defined by Pope Pius XI in his *Quadragesimo Anno*, holds that functions should always be relegated to their most local level possible, lest more distant structures oppress and depersonalize. This principle should be a major point of reference in all of the church's deliberations of structural reform.

15. Philip Turner, "How the Church Might Teach," in *The Crisis in Moral Teaching in the Episcopal Church*, edited by Timothy Sedgwick and Philip Turner (Harrisburg, Pa.: Morehouse Publishing, 1992), pp. 137-159.

16. See John Howard Yoder's *The Priestly Kingdom: Social Ethics as Gospel* (Notre Dame: Notre Dame University Press, 1984), pp. 135-147.

17. Allan Parrent, "On War, Peace, and the Use of Force," in *The Crisis in Moral Teaching in the Episcopal Church*, pp. 94-118 and Turner, "How the Church Might Teach," *The Crisis in Moral Teaching*, pp. 137-159.

18. A poignant description of the end of Christendom can be found in Malcolm Muggeridge's *The End of Christendom* (Grand Rapids: Eerdmans, 1980). Some of the same observations from an Anglican perspective can be found in Lesslie Newbigin's *The Gospel in a Pluralist Society* (Grand Rapids: Eerdmans, 1989).

Part Two

The Challenge of Ministry

Astriking commonality runs through the papers of the St. Louis symposium. Regardless of the perspectives offered, there is general agreement about many of the forces at work within and without the church calling for a re-examination of the church's life. Although many of the authors comment on the serious numerical decline of the mainline churches over the past twenty-five years, most see other trends as far more instructive about the present state and future needs of the church.

The four papers included in this section focus in various ways on the challenges facing the church's ministry in the changing climate of the coming century. They look carefully at a variety of ministry concerns, from the way we staff our national church office to the needs of theological education in the coming century.

Roger J. White, bishop of the diocese of Milwaukee, has had a long involvement with clergy and total ministry development. In the past several years his diocese has piloted the formation of a catechumenal process for the Episcopal Church. Most recently his widely-read book *New Millennium, New Church* (co-authored with Richard Kew) has brought him to the fore in discussions of the church's future shape. Bishop White's paper draws heavily on the monumental Lilly Foundation study of the Presbyterian Church, looking at the present state of "Mainline Protestant America." It sounds a positive note as he discerns trends that lead out of decline toward a renewed strength and mission for the church of the future.

Timothy F. Sedgwick is Professor of Christian Ethics and Moral Theology at Seabury-Western Theological Seminary. He has been deeply active as a lay theologian with particular concerns for the present issues and problems of the church. He has served on a number of councils and commissions of the church, including the Council for the Development of Ministry, and his publications include *The Making of Ministry* and *Sacramental Ethics: Paschal Identity and the Christian Life*. With Philip Turner he edited *The Crisis in Moral Teaching in the Episcopal Church*. Sedgwick's essay here focuses on the problems inherent in the church's present legislative approach to teaching, offering careful analysis and a creative proposal for a more responsible approach in the future.

James L. Fenhagen is the director of the Cornerstone Project of the Episcopal Church Foundation, a national project concerned with the well-being of the clergy and their families. Prior to his current ministry, he was for fourteen years Dean and President of the General Theological Seminary in New York City. He has written four books in the area of spirituality and ministry, including *Invitation to Holiness*. His paper "dreams impossible dreams" that are a genuine challenge for the future of education and ministry in the church.

Peter James Lee is bishop of the diocese of Virginia, one of the oldest, largest, and most varied dioceses in the Episcopal Church. Its 181 congregations include large urban and suburban parishes, African-American, Hispanic, and Korean communities, rural and town churches, congregations oriented toward charismatic renewal, conservative evangelicalism, and Anglo-Catholicism, and many traditional broad church parishes. Bishop Lee's paper is a personal reflection on the ministry and role of the bishop in the future church. His vision places the bishop in the center of the church rather than at the top, thus offering a model for a creative reappropriation of the episcopate in the church of the coming century.

Roger J. White

New Church, New Millennium

I WILL ATTEMPT to achieve three objectives in this presentation. First, I want to share some information about the pathology of Protestant U.S.A. The information comes from a variety of sources, but especially from the Lilly Endowment study developed by the Presbyterian Seminary in Louisville, Kentucky, and focused on the Presbyterian Church, U.S.A.[1] This study has enormous implications for our church. If you don't know where you have been, it is impossible to plan for the future. If you don't know why you don't function the way you want to, or you deny that you are even in need of help, it is impossible to have a vision of what God is calling you to be, never mind trying to see what structures may be helpful to implement that vision. Thus the picture of where we have been is critically important, and its description will make up most of this presentation.

Next, I want to look at some trends that are calling us to restructure our lives as the Episcopal Church, both in the near future and into the new millennium not too far hence. Such trends often give us a clear picture of where the church at its grassroots is heading. Discerning that direction is essential if we are to plan and provide fitting structures to enable God's mission to move ahead.

Finally, I believe that organizational experts are right when they say we shape our structures to fit what has already been envisioned and what is emerging from that vision as it is lived out. Although we don't create our structures so that something in particular may emerge, we do have the flexibility to shape or reshape our structures in the direction we perceive something is emerging. So, what do we need to do to serve the church in mission—to provide structures that support, invigorate, and provide the required resources in an environment that is changing at an ever-increasing rate? I hope in the third part of the presentation to look especially at how the church, renewed, committed, and nurtured at the parish level, enables us to be servants in the whole of creation—to move from self-care and self-concern to being Christ in our world for all God's children.

Where Have We Been?

A major question of the Lilly study of the mainline Protestant church is: "Why is the patient sick?" Although asking this question turns out to be somewhat depressing, hope does emerge if one perseveres! The study documents the fact that Protestant America is in the midst of a major revolution—let me emphasize "in the midst"—and that makes it difficult for us to discern precisely what is happening. The churches are in the process of being reformed, of being reshaped. This is not just tinkering with our life and structures; it is a radical systems change—a paradigm shift—and most of us have no idea that it is happening, no idea what is going on.

The study of the Presbyterian Church points to three major historical moments in the history of Protestant America, three periods of church "disestablishment" in the history of this nation. The first was as the nation was created and the church was legally separated from the state. This separation continues to be a source of debate and conflict in the daily life of the nation and its churches.

In the 1930s, mainline Protestant America became separated—dare we say "aloof"—from much of the rapidly growing culture. The church was seen as somewhat exclusive, certainly very "WASP." The U.S. population swelled with an influx of blue collar immigrants, who were largely ignored by the Protestant churches. This gap has largely remained intact into the present.

In the revolutions of the 1960s the church saw a rapid loss of influence and recognition, power which it had taken for granted for decades. We were separated from our traditional place within the culture. Mainline Protestant America no longer influences the morals, laws, legislation, or direction of the United States to the degree that it once did. It is interesting that many major city newspapers have no religion editor and those who remain are often critical of religion. Clergy once thought of their calling as one of high esteem and low stress; today, it is no exaggeration to say that a minister's vocation is a high stress/low esteem position in many parts of our land. Archbishop George Carey, in his enthronement sermon, reminded the Church of England that she is like a little old lady sitting in the corner making moral and social proclamations: people pat her on the head and then ignore her! Such a description is a fair statement of the change in stature and influence of the church in this country as well. However, in many places, we still live as though it were not so, and deny the fact that radical change has taken place.

No matter how we look at the demographics—everyone interprets them differently—we always have to conclude that the Episcopal Church has sustained a mammoth loss of members in recent decades. During the same time that our nation *grew* by twenty-nine percent we *lost* thirty percent of our members. The Episcopal Church moved from being 1.98 percent of the population to being .98 percent! I don't need to dwell on the obvious, only to say that I am pleased to see that the decline has reached a plateau and in many places churches are growing again or at least recovering.

We need as a part of this analysis to ask, "What are the reasons for such loss?" One reason is an internal confusion as to who we are and what we are about. The Lilly study points to three identity categories of mainline Protestant churches. The first, "secularized churches," are churches that have lost their religious vitality and are basically humanistic with a Christian veneer. Churches that have no unified sense of mission are the second category. They are fragmented into special interest groups that dominate the agenda of the church, leading to a lack of cohesiveness, unity, and direction, and an expenditure of energy on self-interest. The third category describes those who are highly critical of the church itself, critical of the church's witness to the faith—poor leadership, poor formation of adults and children—critical of almost everything the church tries to do. They can be described as those who say, "If only the church had done better, we wouldn't be in this mess today!" These are the naysayers who can only criticize. Since the Episcopal Church is a mix of all three of these categories, it should not be surprising that we have confusion in our sense of direction and a lack of focus on what God calls us to be.

Coupled to this internal strife and confusion is the changed audience to which we are called to appeal. The baby-boomer generation lacks the denominational loyalty of their parents. They have different values. They are much more individualistic and materialistic, and are by-and-large against institutions. When members of this generation return to the church they are selective, wanting the best for their children and for themselves: quality programs, quality facilities, and quality communities. Denominational loyalty and upbringing are a low priority in their choice of churches.

There are other internal factors that have played a role in the decline of membership in the Episcopal Church. We have seen a propensity in our church for it to be very easy to join, easy to be baptized, easy to be confirmed, and then very easy to slide out unnoticed. We have become a church of "easy-in and easy out," with not much expected and not much given. We have become a church of "thin commitment," having a substantial contingency of nominal members and a large and uncommitted fringe.

Along with other mainline Protestant churches, we have been suffering from a malaise caused by self-concern and self-absorption with "in-house" issues, and this malaise has moved us away from an enthusiastic embracing of the mission of the church. Planning and strategy are needed if growth in faith and in numbers is to occur. No plans lead, not surprisingly, to no growth. Self-centeredness and apathy have led us to do some illogical things as a church; for example, at the same time we were losing thirty percent of our membership, we doubled the number of clergy: in 1965 there were seventy-five hundred ordained priests, active and retired, and by 1990 there were fifteen thousand. We have operated our national church and diocesan structures as if nothing has changed for twenty-five years. This denial can be shown by the assessment statistics of one of our eastern dioceses: in 1950 it had 121,000 members; in 1960, 148,000; and by 1990, 75,000. Yet that diocese has only recently begun to adjust its assessment to the Episcopal Church and its methods of staffing, despite such a tremendous decline in membership.

We have come up with few creative approaches to the fact that a parish that once needed two hundred members to support a full-time priest now needs two hundred fifty members if it is to do more than survive. At present, eighty percent of our parishes have memberships of two hundred or less—and yet we still operate on the assumption that each parish needs a full-time priest! We have sat back for twenty-five years and watched rural America move off the farm to the suburbs, and urban America move from the city to the suburbs. We have closed rural and inner city churches, while making little provision for suburban growth.

Some of the root causes in our decline are that we moved from an emphasis on an *individual* relationship to God—being reconciled to God and in turn to one's neighbor—to focus *as a church* on the issues of our society. Most people initially come to the church to establish or reestablish a relationship to Christ. They come to have that "sense" of God's presence in their lives. If that is not there or not emphasized, people do not stay. It is only after they encounter God that they then want to respond and want to be involved in addressing the issues of the world. So often we Episcopalians have lost that first step of *knowing* the God we proclaim—of being right with God. The vacuum we created by missing the first step has been most fruitfully filled by the independent evangelicals. Robert Wuthnow, an astute commentator on Protestant America, observes that we have embraced secularity when we needed to reconcile and convert people so they could address the issues raised by secular society from the strength of their faith.[2] We have not given people the strength of faith needed to address the issues.

Another root cause in our decline has been our move from a focus on education and formation, which were dominant following World War II and through the fifties, to legislation. Education and formation aimed at persuading people. Legislation—often rapidly and poorly drafted and with little or no theological reflection or prayer supporting it—has, on the other hand, been perceived at the grassroots as manipulation from the powers that be, with little or no opportunity to participate in such debate and decision-making.

Perhaps the major shift that has led to our decline, one with which we spend much of our time and energy today, is the shift away from national church program and budget and from diocesan program and strategy to the parish—its mission and ministry. We often behave as if we were a federation of parishes joined into a diocese, and in turn a federation of dioceses joined into the national Episcopal Church. This model is in conflict with the theological belief that holds up the bishop and diocese as the basic unit of the church, a belief which I hold. I do believe, however, that the front line of mission must be the parish because we operate as if the parish is the basic unit of the church. Provide resources to challenge and help that entity, and we will begin to see our vitality rechanneled for the mission of the whole church.

There are other determining factors in the present condition of the church, factors that have either a positive or a negative impact on us: the quality of formation and teaching; the hunger to be fed with good and relevant preaching; the lack of enthusiastic challenges of our young, our old, and our "in-betweens" to give of their lives in service to others; the change from hierarchical models of operation and decision-making to networking and cooperative consensus models of making such decisions; the move to small communities ministering to self and one another, then in turn reaching out to others within the context of the larger church community of which they are very much a part, addressing the needs of the world. We are, I would remind you, "in the midst of the revolution"—we see some things with clarity while others remain hidden and are yet to be revealed. The paradox, as you already know, is that in the midst of the mammoth loss of members there has been renewal, new life, new ways of proclaiming Christ, resulting in thriving and lively communities which give us all hope.

Trends for the Future

This is no time for us as the "New Church" to turn to dust and ashes—to engage in what I call "bashing the bureaucracy." We are resurrection people; we seek the vision of God and then respond by our willingness to be used in fulfilling that vision. Let us admit we have pursued some policies that have been devastating in our lives, and let us then see what God would have us be as the people of God today and tomorrow. So, what are the trends affecting the structures through which we must implement the vision and mission God is giving us?

Many of these trends have already been highlighted by Richard Kew and myself in our book, *New Millennium, New Church*, but let me select some of the pertinent trends that I believe indicate a direction and thus call out for a restructuring which enables us to come closer to being partners in God's mission.

In my estimation, any real change of direction in the life of the church takes at least a generation. Such an assumption makes Larry Rasmussen's musings even more pertinent: a Lutheran theologian at Union Seminary, Rasmussen says we are called to be planters of both pumpkin and date seeds. This is especially true of those in leadership positions in the church. Plant a pumpkin seed and in a short time you see incredible growth and fruitfulness; plant a date seed and it will take a generation to produce its first fruit! We tend more toward pumpkin planting, seeking the instantaneous and impressive, and less toward that which takes time to mature but brings fruitfulness for generations. And yet we need to be planters of both.

The first trend I would point to is a wide variety of *renewal movements* in the life of our church—many seeded twenty or twenty-five years ago. Their focus has been on encountering

Christ in our lives—being fed by God's word and sacraments, nourished in the fellowship and prayer of the spiritual community, and struggling to live out what we profess to believe in word and deed, supported by our relationship to God and Christ and by Christ's body, the church. This renewal has changed and is changing the church, and it needs to be directed and supported as it moves beyond itself to serve all of God's children in the world.

This renewal portion of our membership has moved toward a more centrist stance that tends to find its identity in an orthodoxy based on the description of God found in the creeds of the church. This centrist orthodoxy is grounded in an essential and often life-changing encounter with the God who creates and gives life. It is grounded in an encounter with the God who gives us the means of salvation and reconciliation in Christ Jesus, the God whose living presence sustains, enthuses, and compels us to proclaim the good news of the gospel to all people and with the help of God—and only with that help—to live out what we proclaim. These renewal movements have also stimulated a growing interest in spiritual growth and the formation of individuals in the faith and practice of living the Christian life. This somewhat quiet revolution is, however, demanding of the church. Its demand takes the form of "Feed me—help me grow—or I will find that source, that well of life, where the quenching of my thirst can be found elsewhere!"

In the midst of our confusion in attempting to come to agreement on what God wants us to be and to do, we amazingly have had an enormous *attractiveness to other people*—to those who are lapsed and nonpracticing in their own faith communities and those whose lives have not been shaped by any church. Anglicanism, with its balance and stability, comes shining through for many people who have never encountered such an approach to coming to Christ and serving Christ in their daily living. We offer a balance of evangelical reception of God's word and the stability of sacramental and parish community life. It is a balance which sustains, supports, equips, and nurtures service to Christ and all people and the striving for God's will in this world. Many, I am suggesting, find such a community not only satisfying, but a welcome challenge in which they can be a follower in the Way while dealing honestly with their humanity.

I believe we have neglected—and are at present being called to rectify such neglect—our *understanding and practice of stewardship* of all of God's gifts, from this fragile earth, our island home, to that which we are privileged to steward personally for a little while. Related to this neglect is our introverted focus on ecclesiastical issues, both within our own denomination and within the larger, ecumenical context. Our vision is being expanded and God calls us to be *global in our vision* and attentiveness, not parochial. We are given the resources and knowledge to address the global issues before us. God calls us to be global in the proclamation of the Word and we have retreated to provincialism. The whole world—all God's children—needs to hear the Word proclaimed.

These trends and others which are emerging are setting our future direction. I would be so bold as to say that I believe this is how God works. As we respond to God, often belatedly, we begin to see beyond ourselves as the church to God's mission. Lifting up that vision—addressing that mission—can only move us out of the malaise of our survival mentality and self-concern to be the people of God—ready, willing, and able, with God's help, to do God's will.

Structures for Mission

So what are the structural undergirdings needed to support our response to God's call to be partners in this enormous mission? I believe that is why we are in St. Louis—to raise the vision, to dream dreams, to listen to God, to discern how best to support, to gather resources, to communicate, to come to decisions, and to implement decisions so that the gospel may be proclaimed and lived. What does that mean in specifics?

Certainly it means a reappraisal and clarification of the role of the Presiding Bishop. The task set before the Presiding Bishop has expanded unrealistically. The office functions almost without jurisdiction, with huge responsibility and leadership expectation but with little authority and few supportive mechanisms.

We need a continuing reappraisal and clarification of the role of bishop, priest, and deacon, and the relationship between these orders. The confusion within our understanding of these ministries and their function as related to the whole body of Christians is leading to stress and depression, and continues to be a major source for the lack of motivation and appropriate leadership needed in the church.

We need seriously to reexamine our structures, from the diocese to General Convention and Executive Council; much of what comprises them has a corporate model of management undergirding its ecclesiastical guise. These structures need to be reexamined as to whether they are effective in providing support for the mission of the church. Such evaluation is especially necessary because much of the thinking in the corporate world has reappraised and has radically changed such models of functioning. Yet while the corporate world has changed, the church has been left with an antiquated and often unresponsive structure inhibiting its effective response to be first and foremost focused on preparation for mission and its implementation.

The equipping of people—the support of parish mission and diocesan growth—needs a sharing of expertise: joint and shared planning, both locally and nationally, and the networking of ideas and ways and means. Much of this now happens outside of the formal structure and sometimes in spite of that structure. This is an indication of the inability of the structure to adapt to the emerging direction and thus the needs of the church, especially as it plans and attempts to grow and serve the local community. Such restructuring of program support, resources, and planning needs to be regional—out in the field, with flexibility and with sunset provisions so that we can redirect resources where they are needed and not perpetuate programs for the sake of perpetuating.

Above all—and this may be of some surprise—I believe we need to restructure in order to enable the church, above all else, *to be for others*, as Christ was always the one for others. We need to give ourselves for others that they may know the good news of love, reconciliation, and salvation in and through Jesus Christ.

How can we structure ourselves to tap the vast resources of our people's time, skills, and money? Many of us are doing that outside of the national church structure—look at the missionary societies that challenge and help find resources to go and proclaim the gospel all over the world, when, in theory, the Episcopal Church itself is called the Domestic and Foreign Missionary Society.

We need volunteers, both in our cities and in our countrysides. We need people of many skills, dedicated to Christ—people who are young or retired or on vacation, who want to share their gifts in Christ's name. There are many volunteers who are willing to go where God calls, yet who are left unchallenged. This pool of volunteers needs an undergirding structure to cater to the response as the challenge is given.

So, yes, let us begin with our present structure. Give our Presiding Bishop jurisdiction as called for by Lambeth. Let the Presiding Bishop be a bishop to bishops and dioceses, and let bishops of dioceses be shepherds, pastors, and teachers. Let us utilize the skills of priests, deacons, and laypeople to *administer, implement, equip, build up,* and *enthuse* the church of God for God's mission. Let the General Convention discern God's will for this church. Let the Executive Council adjust and implement the policy, but let us have those who staff and support the church be out in the church—regional, in touch, listening, and flexible enough to change and move on when the task is self-supporting. And above all, let them be sensitive to what God would have us be as the people of God.

Vision or the reception of vision comes out of prayerful discerning of God's will. Implementing the vision often needs structure, communication, and the delivery of resources. Above all, proclaiming the gospel must show that we are caring people whose lives have been transformed and made new and that we are impelled to share such good news. Let us listen, pray, lift the vision, and then, using gifts offered and talents sought out, structure the implementation of those visions that Christ may be known in and through this body called to be servant—not of self, but of Christ.

If we have failed to transmit a compelling Christian message to our children or to anybody else, then we leaders are indeed out of touch with people in the pews. Let us be seekers of God's will, God's way, addressing the enormous hunger for the gospel with integrity, living out the gospel of Christ in word and deed as we serve the real needs of God's people as Christ's servants. We don't need to change the message—just how we structure the conveying and living out of that message. It may not be a new church, but it is to be a new millennium. We are in the midst of what has to date been a quiet revolution, but it is getting noisier and people are showing signs of frustration. Now is the time to listen and to flex—listen, yes to one another, but first to God—and then be brave enough to change, that God's will may be done by you and me and all the church, reshaping and reforming the church for God's mission.

Endnotes

1. The Lilly Endowment study has been published under the series title of *The Presbyterian Presence: The Twentieth-Century Experience*, ed. Milton J. Coalter, John M. Mulder, and Louis B. Weeks (Louisville, Ky.: Westminster/John Knox, 1990).

2. See in particular Wuthnow's *The Restructuring of American Religion: Society and Faith Since World War II* (Princeton N.J.: Princeton University Press, 1988).

Timothy F. Sedgwick

Putting the Church in Scale

One thing seems clear from history and confirmed by daily experience: institutionalism, with its mechanics, never has, and
probably never will, save either the Church or humanity....Un-
der the weight of our increasing machinery or organization, the
conception of the *episcopate* is changing....Our bishops are not
as free as they were to function as the spiritual leaders of their
flocks. More and more they tend to become parts of a hierarchy....It cannot be said too emphatically that the more a
bishop becomes immersed in the details of organization and finance, the less firmly is the Church safeguarding its spiritual
future. The normal result of any mechanical obsession is the
loss of creative spiritual leadership, and this loss will be felt, not
only by the rank and file of the clergy and laity, but also by the
bishops themselves.[1]

I DO NOT KNOW whether or not it is reassuring or cause for a
certain sense of despair, but dissatisfaction and questioning of
the structure of the Episcopal Church is not new. Henry
Davies's description of the Episcopal Church sounds contemporary, but in fact was written in 1926. Perhaps this should
give us cause to pause and first assess our expectations for the
church in order not to fall into some form of utopianism,
whether it be anarchic or communal. Then we might more
coolly view the church and its structure in light of the purposes we seek to accomplish.

   I fear reformist, if not revolutionary, zeal when it is kindled
by a narrow romanticizing of the past, especially an Anglicanism in which the church is the church of the country parson

and the well-knit family. There are in such visions not only a selective reading of the past but also more worrisome assumptions about Christian faith and human possibilities. Larger institutions, both the national church and the dioceses themselves, endanger the life of the church because they are distant and removed from the faith that is given in the congregation.[2] Such an assessment too often rests religiously on a narrow reading of faith in terms of *sola scriptura* or *sola sacramentum*. The new life of Christian faith is mediated quite directly through Scripture or, more likely in Anglicanism, through the sacramental rites of the church; in turn, the new life of faith flows spontaneously in the faithful. The national and diocesan staffs and programs are then suspect to begin with and doubly to be doubted when they appear to be pressing views different from those of the more homogeneous and hence well-knit family of faith. Perhaps no programs elicit such a response more than those addressing human sexuality, though programs raising questions about race or liturgy are also certain to elicit strong reactions.

The critique of the institutionalization of the church as bureaucratic and political is easy. A structure beyond the congregation develops in order to maintain or achieve certain ends. New needs and priorities are pressed by specific groups, even if they are not necessarily shared broadly by the church at large. Staff members and those who serve on the commissions and committees of the church offer their judgments on what needs to be done and develop their own constituencies whom they serve and who support them in their work. New tasks are added, from evangelism and renewal to programs in social ministry. Conflict is inevitable, especially as the church becomes increasingly diverse. And in times when resources are limited, the critique of the larger church can only be expected to increase.

Such critique is necessary and, given the nature of institutions, inevitable. The danger of this critique, however, is that the problems of institutions may so frustrate and anger the people that they cannot articulate and address the larger purposes of the church. These may then be lost from view altogether and replaced by a narrow congregationalism. In this sense, the congregation does evangelism and service; broader needs and possibilities are simply never brought into focus. Constructive change or reform in the church—instead of some kind of sectarian schism—requires more specific, concrete analysis and prescriptions. The question that needs to be addressed is, "Who should do what?" Given the mission or purposes of the church, what can and should be done by congregations and dioceses; and what can and should be done by a separate, national church organization representing and serving these congregations and dioceses?

In addressing such organizational issues of society, Roman Catholic thinkers have developed a principle called "the principle of subsidiarity." This principle states:

> Just as it is gravely wrong to take from individuals what they can accomplish by their own initiative and industry and give it to the community, so also it is an injustice and at the same time a grave evil and disturbance of right order to assign to a greater and higher association what lesser and subordinate organizations can do. For every social activity ought of its very nature to furnish help (*subsidium*) to the members of the body social, and never destroy and absorb them.[3]

This principle applies equally to the church. Individuals and congregations must assume responsibility and initiative for what they alone can do. Commitments of faith, for example, can only be dispositions that reflect and further deepen a person's relationship to God when they are made individually. Faith commitments are compromised or destroyed when they are imposed by the larger community, whether the family, the congregation, or the state acting on behalf of the church. It is for this reason that Roman Catholic and Protestant churches, and even more consistently the Anglican churches, have been clear that above all, the individual must follow his or her own conscience. The church is to educate and provide pastoral support, but the decisions that reflect a person's fundamental convictions and values must be made by the individual him or herself.

In turn, decisions for the common good—or ecclesially we may say for the sake of the Body of Christ—cannot be made individually, as if the sum of individual decisions was sufficient to form and shape the church. The very commitment to episcopal leadership is a commitment to an apostolic faith, a faith that has a history which is borne in particular ways by persons ordained for the sake of the whole church. Bishops, for example, are educated and given power and authority for shaping the doctrine and discipline (or we might say the teaching and mission) of the church so that the church remains faithful to its identity in Christ. Now, of course, bishops do not act unilaterally, or at least when they do their authority is diminished. Teaching and discipline arise as well from the broad experience of the whole church and the expertise of particular members. Nonetheless, while individuals alone can make decisions of conscience, a larger structure encompassing ordained offices is assumed to be necessary for accomplishing other purposes. The question in assessing the church, its structure, and its future then remains, "Who should do what?" In other words, what can and should be done by congregations and dioceses; and what can and should be done by a separate, national church organization representing and serving these congregations and dioceses?

Present Structure

The structure that carries out the work of the church as a national church is not primarily a matter of the triennial meetings of the General Convention, with its House of Bishops and House of Deputies, or even the Presiding Bishop and the Executive Council who are to implement the decisions of General Convention and act on the church's behalf. Even the House of Bishops, which usually meets once a year, is not the primary body in carrying out the work of the church as a national church. Rather, the structure of the national church is given by the commissions and committees created by the General Convention and the professional staff who, while serving at the pleasure of the Presiding Bishop, are the professional bureauc-

racy that carries out particular programs and serves the commissions and committees. This structure is important to keep
in mind because any changes in "who should do what" will require changes in legislative, executive, and administrative functions in these bodies.

The work itself of the national church may be conceived in
terms of internal and external activities. Some of the work is
internal to the Episcopal Church: for example, governance, liturgical change, teaching, congregational development, and the
development of the mission and ministry of the church. Other
work of the national church is external to congregations in the
sense that the work represents or acts on behalf of congregations as a whole in relationship to others. This includes ecumenical relations, world mission, and world relief aid. In terms
of the principle of subsidiarity, some of these purposes must be
assumed by a national church structure.

To have an identity that is more than congregational requires a staff and structure to govern the common life in such
matters as ordination, the formation of new dioceses, and provisions for insurance, disability, and pensions. A common life
also requires the development of common music and liturgies,
as represented in the Book of Common Prayer and the Hymnal.
Provision for foreign mission, including financial and educational resources for other churches in the Anglican Communion, likewise requires coordination at a national level. No
doubt, dioceses and congregations may enter into other relationships, such as the companion relationships between many
dioceses and other churches in the Anglican Communion. But
even this requires some national coordination. In turn, while
congregations and dioceses may provide money, people, and
other resources for the aid of others—from a cathedral shelter
for the homeless to tutoring immigrants in English as a second
language to legal aid and advocacy—a national church structure with staff is necessary for the appeal and coordination of
some such aid, especially internationally. The Presiding
Bishop's Fund for World Relief has served the Episcopal Church
in this way. Finally, in order to seek unity and common witness of faith the Episcopal Church has entered into a range of

ecumenical relationships. Such work—the bilateral dialogues
with other denominations such as Lutherans, Roman Catholics, and Orthodox, for example—needs to be undertaken and
coordinated at a national level.

No doubt in each of these areas—governance, hymnody and
liturgy, foreign mission, world relief, and ecumenical relations—changes in the national church structure may be recom-
mended. But whatever changes may be considered, it is
difficult to imagine the Episcopal Church able to achieve its
purposes as a national church apart from something of the present commissions and committees established by General Convention and the professional staff needed to support this work.
While not without controversy, this work is most generally
supported. The work most contested is that done in teaching,
in congregational development, and in development of mission
and ministry of the church within the United States.

The commissions and committees established by General
Convention for the development of mission and ministry include the Standing Commissions on the Church in Metropolitan Areas, on the Church in Small Communities, on
Evangelism, on Health, on Human Affairs, on Peace and Justice, and on Stewardship and Development; and the Joint
Commission on AIDS. The professional staff with responsibilities in these areas has been organized in terms of two divisions
of the program group at the Episcopal Church Center: Advocacy, Witness, and Justice Ministries, and Education, Evangelism, and Ministry Development. Some thirty staff members
have particular responsibilities for program in areas such as
Asian American, African American, Hispanic, and Native
American ministries; women in mission and ministry; rural
and small town ministries; refugee and immigration ministries;
AIDS ministries; peace and justice ministries; public policy;
congregational development; evangelism; children and young
adult ministries; and adult education and leadership training.

Some of the work in what is called the "program group" of
professional staff may only be done or may be best coordinated
at the national level. This may well be the case for what are
called the development of ethnic ministries or for furthering

the development of AIDS ministries as established by the General Convention in 1988. But, however good the causes may be or however important the work of staff members may be, the question remains, "To what extent does such work represent and serve the church as a whole?" Or, more pointedly and critically, "What are the ends and purposes intended and how does the structure support the participation in these ends by the church as a whole, specifically dioceses and congregations?" The answer to these questions is not given in terms of some first principles. The church could order its structure and resources in quite different ways, for example, to provide for teaching and education. But, unless such structure is clear and communicated, assessment, support, and reorganization are impossible, and alienation, frustration, and anger are the consequences. Such is the attitude of large segments of the Episcopal Church, at least toward the two program divisions of the Episcopal Church staff identified as Advocacy, Witness, and Justice Ministries and Education, Evangelism, and Ministry Development.

Problems in a Quasi-Legislative Structure

The difficulty of the national church in education, congregational development, and ministry programs is that priorities and programs themselves become highly political and partisan. Individuals on commissions and committees, or ad hoc task forces, for example, press for adoption of their particular views on the teaching of the church. This has certainly been the case on the Standing Commissions on Health, on Human Affairs, and on Peace and Justice. Attempts to ensure broad representation of provinces, minorities, women and men, and those with differing points of view creates the impression for commissions, committees, and staffs alike that through their reports and resolutions they are expressing the mind of the church as they seek to form and shape it. We then have reports and resolutions on everything from the nature of homosexuality to pacifism and the nuclear arms race, from abortion to justice and American health care.

As David Smith and Judith Granbois assess the teaching of the church, the problem is "thinking in terms of the quasi-legislative mode and formulating resolutions." As reflected in the Church of England, what is needed is "a better, if slower, way of responding" in which a variety of persons and working groups would develop teaching materials for the church. In short, "the problem is structural and fundamental."[4] And what is true of teaching is all the more true at the national church in undertaking particular programs, whether in evangelism or to support women in their lives and increase their participation in the church. To seek strategic programs through representative commissions and committees is to assume a hierarchical form of authority that runs counter not only to Anglican tradition but to the actual polity of the Episcopal Church. This, of course, has its irony in that many program initiatives seek to be inclusive and to overcome what is perceived as the oppressive hierarchy of the past. Such programs, like reports and resolutions that address matters of the teaching of the church, are not only often divisive and result in the withdrawal of support for the national church staff and structure, they fail to effect a broad participation of the individuals and congregations of the church.

Again, criticism is easier than constructing structures that would enable initiatives to respond to needs in education, in congregational development, and in the development of the mission and ministry of the church. In order to avoid easy criticism or abstract and idealized proposals, I want to focus on the task of the national church in teaching and, in this light, make specific proposals for restructuring present authority and responsibilities.

A New Structure for Teaching

Teaching should be understood as ordinarily happening throughout the church, for example, by individual persons, congregations and dioceses, voluntary associations (such as Associated Parishes or Episcopalians United), publishers and publications (ranging from *The Witness* to Forward Movement,

Cowley, and Morehouse), theological seminaries, and diocesan schools. A variety of voices raise consciousness of new concerns and understandings. A range of perspectives on the Christian tradition enable the appropriation of the tradition. Different judgments and prescriptions are offered. Consensus develops slowly on points of agreement and on those matters about which Christians disagree. Such teaching is what has been traditionally referred to as the ordinary magisterium. Ways to identify and support such teaching in order to make it broadly available to the church at large are certainly important, but what may be most important is affirming that most teaching happens in this ordinary way and does not require the work of a national church.

Some national structure for the church, though, is needed to identify and address issues that are essential to the integrity of the church as a national church in the Anglican Communion. On some matters of doctrine and discipline the church as a national body larger than congregations and dioceses needs to identify, address, and, where necessary, resolve the issues that threaten to divide the church. Resolution of areas of disagreement need not demand uniformity of understanding. As in the case of the question of the use of force—that is to say the question of whether Christians should be pacifist or not—the church may claim that different views may be faithful understandings of the nature and demand of faith. Issues that have or continue to demand such attention include the ordination of women, the theology and use of the 1979 Book of Common Prayer, and understandings of evangelism, abortion, and homosexuality. Such teaching, structured to give expression to understandings that are or need to be shared by the church as a whole, has been designated as matters of the extraordinary magisterium.

As the church addresses particular issues, more fundamental questions regarding understandings of Christian faith may be raised. More than resolving differences over particular issues, teaching may be needed to provide broader understandings of what is central to Christian faith. While this may often be best accomplished through the ordinary magisterium, there may be times when the church as a whole needs to speak. Teaching, for example, on holy orders, the authority of Scripture, the renewal of the catechumenate, or the nature of ministry might be appropriately developed at a national level in order to prompt and deepen shared understandings.

There are also outstanding challenges to the community of faith that may need to be addressed for the sake of the unity and integrity of the church in its life and witness, perhaps especially those challenges the church needs to address in order to bear witness to Christ in the world. The Roman Catholic bishops, for example, have exercised strong leadership in their church in placing before the community of faith and the nation itself questions regarding the use of nuclear weapons and basic responsibility for economic justice.[5] They have provided teaching that summarizes the consensus as well as the diversity of understandings and convictions in the Christian community. In this light they have provided a prophetic voice raising issues that must be addressed. They have also deepened understandings of faith and informed conscience by indicating basic Christian teachings and convictions, as well as by exploring what remains problematic where persons of good faith may disagree.

Instead of the present quasi-legislative model with its politics of representation, coalitions, and compromise, developing a more adequate national structure for teaching—we might say developing the structure for the extraordinary magisterium in the Episcopal Church—requires clear responsibility for teaching from persons accountable to and representative of the church at large. In turn, the problems created by forming a bureaucracy of professionals who develop and serve particular constituencies must be avoided. In this light, the present problems in the area of teaching arise from the different priorities pressed by different groups—from General Convention, the representatives to commissions and committees and their constituencies, professional staff, and the Presiding Bishop himself. Alternatively, the bishops should assume responsibility for teaching.

In developing a structure for the extraordinary magisterium I would propose that some of the Standing Commissions and Committees of the General Convention be dissolved: for example, the Standing Commissions on Health, on Human Affairs, and on Peace and Justice. This is not to say that the issues that these commissions have addressed are not important. Rather, these commissions do not provide the appropriate structure to develop effective teaching at the national level. In fact, they may prevent establishing priorities because they press before the church issues under their purview rather than enabling a broader assessment of what is needed in light of available resources. Instead, the House of Bishops should assume responsibility for teaching at the national level. For example, a House of Bishops' committee on teaching and ministry might well be established to make recommendations to the House for teaching. The process itself of addressing what is needed would help the bishops assume responsibility for the common life of the church.

In terms of providing teaching, the House of Bishops would then have available to them a variety of possibilities. They might seek to develop a written document similar to what the Roman Catholic bishops have called pastoral teaching. This would require staff support, consultations, and public forums. Education would arise from the process of developing the teaching as well as from the use of the final document. Alternatively, the bishops might request a small group of persons to prepare materials from which they would construct a more modest report or teaching for the church. Or, the bishops might simply request a variety of persons to prepare materials without seeking to develop a document assuming to speak for and to the church as a whole. Much of such teaching might then well be done by dioceses individually or cooperatively or by one of the nine provinces of the Episcopal Church.

Funding for this work should come from the church, specifically the dioceses, in light of the budgets approved by General Convention. I would suggest that funding for the work of the House of Bishops be proposed by the House of Bishops and approved by the House of Deputies. Presently, as reported by the

Standing Commission on the Structure of the Church in its report to the 1991 General Convention, "almost all of the annual budget of each [commission] is spent on travel, lodging and meal expenses in connection with meetings of the group."[6] This in itself makes nearly impossible the development and use of resources necessary for informed teaching, much less for education, or what Roman Catholics call the promulgation of teachings. In turn, presently the House of Bishops has limited or no budget from the General Convention for its work. Together the change in initiating teaching by placing responsibility with the House of Bishops, the elimination of certain commissions and committees and professional staff, and giving responsibility to the House of Bishops for proposing budgets and funding while placing the approval of budgets and funding with the House of Deputies suggests a structure that would provide for accountability, encourage the development of priorities, and make possible adequate funding for the limited work that can be undertaken.

Similar Changes in Ministry

This proposal focusing on teaching in the church may be extended to address how the church at a national level should address congregational development and the developing of the mission and ministry of the smaller units of the church, the dioceses and congregations. As with teaching, members of standing commissions and committees assume responsibility for representing different constituencies and perspectives. They then seek to give direction to programs that they believe are important for the development of the ministry and the mission of the church. In this area, more than in teaching, program for ministry development is assumed by professional staff members.

As in teaching, questioning the present structuring of the national church is not to question the value of work that is now done. Rather, my question of the present structure is in order to address the question of what structure may enable the assessment and accountability necessary to prevent an uncritical bureaucratic structure and enable the establishment of clear priorities. We must always ask, "What can and needs to be done at the national level for the sake of the congregations and dioceses of the church?" And, "What is to be done or must be done at the national level because only a national structure can respond on behalf of the church or because only a response from a national structure can better enable the participation of the whole church?" Here in ministry areas, as in teaching, I would dissolve the standing commissions and committees that now assume oversight and eliminate professional staff positions. In the place of this current structure, I would give the initiative for beginning and continuing particular programs with the House of Bishops while leaving the approval of budgets to the House of Deputies.

Placing responsibility for oversight over teaching and ministry at the national level with the House of Bishops is no panacea ensuring the principle of subsidiarity—that every action will be undertaken to furnish help to individuals, congregations, and dioceses and not destroy their initiative and participation in the mission of the church. But at least accountability is clear, priorities must be assessed, and the case for undertaking a particular course of action must be made to and supported by the larger church as represented in the House of Deputies.

What is surprising—or perhaps simply evidence of the problems of the present structure of the national church—is that no such concrete proposals have been proposed and broadly discussed, though the Standing Commission on the Structure of the Church has as its goal for this triennium to review "the whole relationship of General Convention, the Executive Council and its professional staff."[7] There are surely other ways of restructuring responsibility and authority for the national church in order to achieve these ends. What is needed, however, are concrete proposals on structure in terms of the purposes of the national church and the principle of subsidiarity. Such work may not be as stirring as critiques of power and perspectives or as suggestive as discussions of new trends and signs of reformation. But, without such specificity critics will only serve to further alienation and anger and finally schism within the Episcopal Church or, at best, to further a distinctly Protestant congregationalism.

Endnotes

1. Henry Davies, "The Future of the Episcopal Church in America," *Anglican Theological Review* IX (July 1926) 1:10-12.

2. The national church and the Episcopal Church in the United States of America (ECUSA) are unfortunate designations in that the provinces of the Episcopal Church are not circumscribed by the national borders of the United States but include other countries. (Province IX is comprised of countries of Central America.) The term "national church" is, though, used to designate the structure that represents and works on behalf of dioceses. The term "Episcopal Church" designates the church as a whole, including congregations, dioceses, provinces, and "national" structures.

3. *Quadragesimo Anno* (On Reconstructing the Social Order), para. 79, published in *The Church and the Reconstruction of the Modern World: The Social Encyclicals of Pius XI*, ed. Terence P. McLaughlin (Garden City, N.J.: Image, 1957), p. 247.

4. David Smith and Judith Granbois, "New Technologies for Assisted Reproduction," *The Crisis in Moral Teaching in the Episcopal Church*, ed. Timothy F. Sedgwick and Philip Turner (Harrisburg, Pa.: Morehouse Publishing, 1992), pp. 50-51.

5. See the National Conference of Catholic Bishops, *The Challenge of Peace* (Washington, D.C.: U.S. Catholic Conference, 1983) and the National Conference of Catholic Bishops, *Economic Justice for All* (Washington, D.C.: U.S. Catholic Conference, 1986).

6. The Standing Commission on the Structure of the Church, *The Blue Book* (Phoenix, Ariz., 1991), p. 488.

7. Ibid., p. 496.

James C. Fenhagen

Educating Leaders for the Church

LET ME BEGIN my remarks by expressing to the planners of this symposium my appreciation for being asked to participate in what certainly is a new kind of "happening" in the Episcopal Church. It is exciting to be with a group of people who are interested in moving beyond our seemingly endless discussions about what we perceive to be wrong with the Episcopal Church in order that we might think together as concerned Christians about how we might respond faithfully and courageously to the future which confronts us. We are living in what some have referred to as a "culture of complaint," where as a nation and as a church our tendency is to use our energy and our passion more on finding someone to blame—be it the President, or the Presiding Bishop, or the liberals, or the conservatives—rather than helping to find solutions. This symposium, however, as I understand it, is about dreaming "impossible dreams," in the faith that no dream, when touched by the Spirit, is impossible.

The concern of this forum is theological education at every level of the church's life. I speak to you as one whose whole ministry in one way or another has been concerned with this subject. I have served as a seminary dean, as a diocesan director of Christian education, as a parish priest, and more specifically, as a believing Christian whose faith has been nourished, deepened, and challenged by the educational ministries of countless clergy and laity over the years who have shared their faith with me. Having said this, however, let me share with you the bias that underlies this presentation. I believe that the ongoing education of the people of God in the meaning of faith and ministry in our time is critical to the church's future. The qualities that make effective leaders are gifts of the Spirit, but they are gifts that need to be nurtured, deepened, and challenged. To give in to the anti-intellectual bias that dominates so much religious thinking in our day, to settle for easy answers to the hard questions that the world presents to us, to speak before we have engaged in the hard task of listening to someone else, is to diminish the gifts that we have been given and that the church so badly needs.

With this bias clearly stated, let me dare to dream some "impossible dreams." I would like to explore with you three areas related to the educational task of the church that I believe need some honest rethinking. These three areas have to do with education and our baptismal covenant; seminary education; and education as a mission imperative to children and youth. Alan Jones, in a stimulating article in the *Sewanee Theological Review*, writes that "Christianity is a work of the imagination before it is a set of dogmatic propositions."[1] We will need this sense of openness with its wonder and expectancy if the Spirit is to change us as individuals and as a church.

Education and the Baptismal Covenant

First of all, the baptismal covenant is God's invitation to us to share in the ministry of Jesus Christ. To make this ministry possible we are incorporated into the risen life of Christ himself. We live in him as he lives in us. This is why prayer and worship and the study of Scripture are so central to the Christian life. These are the ways life in Christ is deepened and sustained, and it is from this root that we become Christ-bearers for others. God through the Holy Spirit penetrates our lives through the water of baptism. A process of transformation begins through which Jesus Christ becomes the dominant reality in the way we think, in what we see, and in the way we respond to the world around us. This is what Paul was talking about when he said, "I have been crucified with Christ; and it is no longer I who live, but it is Christ who lives in me" (Gal.

2:19-20). This is the arena in which all our conversations with each other must take place. This is the reality to which all of our educational efforts must respond. As we confront the world that is emerging, these are the essential truths that we must bring with us. This is what binds us together. "Christ has died. Christ has risen. Christ will come again."

Secondly, if we are to enter into the baptismal covenant at a level where the transforming power of the Spirit can be experienced and appropriated, participation in a regular, disciplined small group can no longer be seen as an activity limited to the superpious or the excessively needy. It is a way of sharing in the Christ-life that is as normative as Sunday morning worship. This is not something new, but the reality of its importance as a fundamental discipline of the Christian life is new for the church at large. The content and shape of the group is not so important as the commitment to some disciplined way of engaging the gospel story with a group of people whom we trust enough to share something of our journey in faith. For some, Cursillo has met this need. For others, it is an Education for Ministry group or a group that meets for Bible study and prayer. The point is, the experience that an ongoing group can provide is necessary if we are to move from a church of consumers to a church of participants. My dream is that God will take what is already going on and make it central to the life of every congregation in our church, no matter how large or how small.

And lastly, if we are to take the educational task of our baptismal covenant seriously we must come to see the church not as a hierarchical community with power centered at the top, but as a community of many ministries where power is affirmed in accordance with need. In the last twenty-five years we have seen a major theological shift in the Episcopal Church. With the emphasis in the 1979 Prayer Book on the centrality of the sacrament of baptism, the ministry of the laity has taken on new meaning and new authority. However, this new emphasis has created a theological time lag. Our theology of ordination and the symbols that support it simply have not kept pace with the Holy Spirit's leading in the church. What is needed is an understanding of ordination that is catholic without being authoritarian and that views leadership not as something separate or distinct from the community of faith, but as something that is affirmed and empowered from within. The ordained person is not someone set apart, but someone set within the community of faith as a sign of what we are all called to be. To accept this will mean a willingness to examine the titles we give to one another to see if they honestly describe what we believe. It will mean that clergy will transfer into a parish just as laity do. It will mean revisions in our liturgies for ordination that communicate what we are seeking to affirm. As we approach the twenty-first century we are being asked to think in new ways about who we are in relation to one another. We are being asked to listen to voices in our midst that we have not heard before. We are being invited to claim the authority of our baptism in ways that change the way the church looks and acts, for this is what the call to mission is about.

Seminary Education

There are eleven accredited seminaries in the Episcopal Church. Four are located in the first and second provinces of the church, three others in the third and fourth provinces, with the remaining four in provinces five, seven, and eight. It is generally accepted in the church that we have too many seminaries. Any kind of graduate educational institution is very expensive to maintain and resources in the church are becoming more and more scarce. We all know that this is true, but what we have had trouble facing is that there is no magic wand, or national body, that can reduce the number of seminaries in accordance with a formula honoring the diversity and emphasis that each of our seminaries represent. Each seminary in our church is an independent institution governed by a board of trustees. They will close or merge when forced to by the economic realities that confront them. The issue, therefore, is not how many seminaries, but rather, how can the seminaries be more closely related to the church at large?

So, for a start, I would like to see every diocese in the church have a direct seminary connection. In some cases this connection would be based on geography, in other cases, shared theological emphasis, or in most cases, a mixture of both. I would like to see the seminaries involved in baptismal education and the continuing education of the clergy in a disciplined way that emerges out of joint planning and joint staffing. Why could not a liaison person be established, whose salary was underwritten jointly and whose ministry would involve building and sustaining the kind of connections that are so badly needed? I would like to see a system set up whereby participating dioceses could have some impact on the curriculum in the seminaries. There is wisdom in the church at large that is never heard in the seminary community, much less made use of. There is wisdom in the seminaries that is never really drawn upon in the church at large. This is one of the issues we must deal with if we are to use the educational resources that are available to us. There are connections between seminaries and dioceses or seminaries and congregations already in place, but we have a long way to go if these connections are to build the kind of mutuality and trust that we so badly need.

Secondly, I dream that the organizing principle for the curriculum of study in our seminaries be a serious emphasis on education for leadership in the life of the church—education that would address the ministries of both clergy and laity and involve both in the process itself. What the church needs as it faces the future are men and women able to accept the responsibilities of leadership and able to lead. This should be the organizing principle around which seminary curriculums are built. What do men and women need to know to serve as theological leaders in a post-Christian society? What do they need to know and *be* as builders of communities of faith? Seminaries need not only to impart knowledge, but equally to help women and men share with others what they have come to know for themselves. All of the seminaries, in one way or another, are concerned with this issue, but to my mind reinforcing and deepening the gifts of leadership given to us by the

Spirit needs to be more clearly articulated as the center of the theological education enterprise.

Finally, if seminaries are to take seriously the kind of ordained leadership that is needed for the church—that is, clergy who see themselves as set within, rather than set apart—the task of constructing a theology of ordination that keeps pace with our theology of baptism must be seen as an issue of critical importance. To confront this issue, however, will involve more than theological inquiry and debate. It will mean addressing the culture of the seminary itself. How can we train leaders for a church that is seeking to discover what it means to be less hierarchical in an atmosphere where hierarchy, for the most part, reigns supreme? While I do indeed believe that academic communities need the freedom to explore new ideas and test old ones without the fear of job loss because someone might disagree, I wonder if there are not ways to ensure this safety without the current dependence on a tenure system that models the very opposite of what the church understands itself to be.

All of our seminaries need to determine what kind of educational community will best reinforce the mutuality that leadership in the church now requires. The challenge this poses for the seminaries of our church is exciting and not easily resolved, but will be a concern that touches every aspect of the church's life in the years to come.

The Education of Children as a Mission Imperative

In her recent novel, *The Children of Men*, P. D. James describes in apocalyptic terms a world where there are no longer any children. Twenty-five years before the narrative in the novel begins, human fertility comes to an end. Children's playgrounds are boarded up. Women are seen pushing dressed up animals in baby carriages, and the world's inhabitants grow older and more and more dependent on the authority of government to ease the pain. What we see in P. D. James's world, of course, is a parable of our own. It is a world which epitomizes the ultimate rejection of children—yet is a world which in theological terms requires a child to save it.

Despite all the rhetoric to the contrary, we live in a society that has to a large degree abandoned its children. We are interested in children if they belong to us, while we are blind to the pain of those children who live outside our range of comfort. We view the steady decline of children in our churches and the loss of our youth as if we were helpless to do anything about it. And as a nation we respond to the rapidly deteriorating social structures that support children in our nation's cities as if it were someone else's problem, if we respond at all. The fate of the world's children, and their God-given right to grow up in a world that cares for their future, is a mission imperative for the twenty-first century that is staring us in the face.

In a provocative book chapter entitled, "Welcoming Children in My Name," Fredrica Harris Thompsett points out that, according to the 1990 census, one in four Americans under the age of eighteen lives below the poverty line. "This country may now be first in the number of billionaires," Dr. Thompsett notes, but, "sadly, we also come first among industrial nations in childhood poverty."[2] And when you look beyond our own nation to those children growing up in the third world, you realize the massive dimensions of the problem.

Welcoming children—ours and other people's—in the name of the Lord involves more, of course, than being sensitized to the effects of mass poverty on children. It involves what and how we teach our children about human differences, about prejudice, and about treating other persons with decency and respect. And it involves making the commitment necessary for our churches to be places where children are welcome.

What would it mean if we made ministry to children and youth our major mission priority for the next decade? What would happen if we linked up with other groups and other churches to see that teachers in the community were honored and supported? What would it mean if resources were targeted so that every church building in the Episcopal Church housed a preschool program with support services for children? What if our budgets gave priority to youth ministry and the work of our church on college campuses? We might not like the way the Southern Baptists or the Assemblies of God do things, but when it comes to children and youth, they are light years ahead of the Episcopal Church, and their numbers reflect it. If we really got serious about our children—and other people's children—we might learn something about ourselves and the kind of church we are called to be.

Taking the Next Step

Christian leadership is a call from God to share in the servant ministry of Jesus Christ. It is a call, however, which can be easily distorted and misused because of our failure to develop and deepen the gifts we have been given. In a superb little monograph entitled "Leading from Within," Parker Palmer writes:

> A leader is a person who has an unusual degree of power to project on other people his or her shadow, or his or her light. A leader is a person who has an unusual degree of power to create the conditions under which other people must live and move and have their being....A leader is a person who must take special responsibility for what's going on inside him or her self, inside his or her consciousness, lest the act of leadership create more harm than good.[3]

If the Episcopal Church is to be responsive to the challenge offered to it, we must have leaders whose lives are deeply rooted in Jesus Christ and open to the Spirit in ways that allow them to listen from their hearts. We need leaders who can contribute to the building of communities of faith where Christ is known and where the world is served in his name. We need leaders who see children and youth in all their possibility and wonder, and who are willing to try new ways of solving old problems.

Educating leaders for the twenty-first century is fundamental to the mission of the church. It touches every aspect of the church's life because the growth that education produces is a sign of the presence of the Spirit in our midst. Thank you for listening to my dreams. I look forward now to hearing some of yours as we prepare ourselves as a church to take the next step.

Endnotes

1. Alan Jones, "The New Millennium: Pastoral Care in Apocalyptic Times," *Sewanee Theological Review* 36:3 (Pentecost 1993), p. 305.

2. Fredrica Harris Thompsett, *Courageous Incarnation* (Boston: Cowley Publications, 1993), p. 43.

3. Parker J. Palmer, *Leading from Within: Reflections on Spirituality and Leadership* (Washington, D.C.: Servant Leadership School, 1990), p. 5.

Peter James Lee

A Bishop in the Church of God

MY MOTHER WILL BE eighty-five years old in a few weeks and she still has much to teach me, as she reminds me from time to time. She certainly taught me something on the day I was elected a bishop. My older brother and I have been involved with the church since before we can remember and he continues to offer leadership in his ministry as a lay person in a parish in Houston, Texas. I was surprised by my election and I wanted to share the news with my family. So I called mother and told her, "Mother, I've just been elected Bishop of Virginia." Mother responded sweetly, "That's nice, son. Your brother has just been elected to the vestry of St. John the Divine in Houston."

Mother had it right. Both of her sons exercise ministries in the church, ministries of governance: one on a vestry and another in the episcopate. Both ministries are essential and yet both are secondary to the ministry of the Body of Christ in the world. Mother had it right because the ministries of all baptized people are important. The most important ministries we have, however, are representing Christ in the world. Secondary ministries we share are the ministries of strengthening, empowering, and nurturing the church for that primary mission. How we govern the church is not as important as how we proclaim the gospel and serve God's people in the world. Sometimes we get our wires crossed and think government is more important than mission.

I spend a great deal of time as a bishop maintaining what is. My Sunday calendar is fixed some eighteen months in advance.

I can tell you now what churches I will be visiting next year. I do not criticize our capacity to schedule in advance. Scheduling is essential if congregations are to plan effectively in the long term so that adult converts to the faith can be baptized when the bishop visits at the end of a long process of preparation. Scheduling is essential if bishops are to be truly representative persons, visiting the wide range of congregations in their dioceses, encouraging the ministries of all the baptized in the world.

Nonetheless, Sunday by Sunday, it feels more like maintenance than mission. There are exceptions. It was a wonderful experience a few weeks ago to visit a new congregation that meets in a multiplex theater. We used no prayer books, no hymnals. The full text of every hymn and every word of the liturgy—without breaking a single rubric—were flashed on the silver screen. The congregation could participate with their heads up, making eye contact with their bishop and with one another as they kept up with the service on the screen. It was a modern experience of a post-literate age, the church on a mission in the world. The only drawback was walking into the theater (vested in my sixteenth-century, House of Lords parliamentary dress) past a sign that said, "Indecent Proposal Rated R." The images were a little hard to integrate! But maybe that is part of mission; being a people immersed in the world who do not quite fit in because our loyalties are finally elsewhere, and not of this world.

Much of a bishop's present work in the church is based on maintaining what is: recruiting sufficient clergy to fill positions in congregations that want more than they can pay for; indicating to clergy and their families that a bishop is a pastor, able and willing to listen patiently to them as they go through the inevitable pressures of living in a confusing time. Some people expect their bishops to voice with clarity the particular passions of one side or another within the church. And some are deeply disappointed when their bishops refuse that claim. What we expect of our bishops at present is clearly more than any one person can or should produce.

A recent diocesan profile of a diocese that expects to elect a bishop in a few months listed these elements as a result of their diocesan-wide survey:

> [The] clergy and laity want their bishop to have a deep personal relationship with Jesus Christ and to be open in sharing that faith...a person who is compassionate and caring and [who] possesses leadership and pastoral skills which will be used effectively with clergy and laity...a knowledgeable and effective preacher...one who exercises leadership within the wider church as well as in public issues in the secular community...[one who has] knowledge and understanding of liturgy, apostolic authority, faith and practice...[who is] genuinely concerned about the personal welfare of clergy and clergy families. Qualities basic to these concerns are respect for individual, racial and cultural differences. The bishop must be honest, trusting, and very accessible to the congregations but practice confidentiality when appropriate....The bishop must have [the ability] to articulate a clear vision and constancy of purpose, create a climate of harmony, pastor clergy and their families...one who will proclaim intentional advocacy of the ministry of the laity...one who will seek involvement in the church beyond the diocesan level.

After listing these elements, this same profile went on to identify several areas to which they hoped the new bishop would give attention, including adult Christian education and educational ministries, Sunday school, clergy continuing education, vocational development, the promotion of renewal ministries, and meeting the needs of older persons. This same profile indicated areas needing attention of the bishop to be assisting rural and small town ministries and providing for a broader inclusions of minorities.

That profile, developed by a serious, conscientious, and inclusive committee, is very similar to many profiles that I see. Can anyone expect to meet those expectations? Look at them closely and they add up to a list for maintenance—maintaining everybody's agenda—more than focusing on a few clear claims for mission.

What is the reality that a bishop faces? A typical week for me might begin with a telephone call to the chancellor on a new allegation of sexual misconduct by one of the clergy. The same day might include a meeting with a priest who is profoundly unhappy with the Episcopal Church and wishes to leave. It might include an appeal from a diocesan committee that needs more money than the budget provides, or an urgent call from an ecumenical colleague who wants sponsorship by statewide church leaders for a public policy initiative, or a meeting with members of a mission committee unhappy with decisions made concerning their vicar. It is likely to include meetings with clergy who are candidates for vacant positions in the diocese. And where in this day does the bishop find time or make time for a fresh new sermon that is based on the lectionary, suitable to the particular concerns of the three different congregations where the bishop will preach that week, a sermon that will be personally engaging as the bishop shares his or her life with the people, and reflective of his or her own spiritual depth and growing awareness of the richness of the biblical narrative?

The diocesan profile that I quoted points both to the weakness and the strength of the present use of the episcopate. Our strength is that we use the episcopate to personify ministry. I believe this to be a fundamental strength of the Episcopal Church. Our basic symbols of leadership are not committees or conventions, but persons. And yet we sum up in an agenda for the bishop everyone else's agenda in the church. What we are doing is confusing symbol with function, just as we have confused leadership with management. The bishop is a symbol of what the church has been, of who it is now, and what it will become in Christ's future. That is why a bishop has both horizontal and vertical dimensions in his or her world. The bishop personifies apostolic succession, not through some literalist transmission of hands on heads, nor through some wooden recital of the slogans of an earlier generation, but rather in living communion with the church across the ages. The bishop represents the continuity of the apostles' teaching and fellowship that is the first promise we make in the baptismal covenant as a consequence of our belief in the living Christ. That vertical dimension of the bishop's ministry across history is imperiled when the episcopate becomes idiosyncratic, defined primarily by the winds of change of a particular generation.

A bishop in touch with the role of symbolic transmission of apostolic identity will respect the peculiar, unmodern character of that dimension of ministry, and will avoid the trap of meeting the claims of everyone else in a particular generation. Such a bishop will reject a role as a micromanager of detail. As one who symbolizes and embodies continuity, the bishop stands at the intersection of past, present, and future as a leader of the people for the present to lead them into God's future.

I am very aware that I am the twelfth bishop of the diocese of Virginia. It was a powerful experience for me in September 1990 to participate in a Eucharist in the chapel of Lambeth Palace, London, the very same chapel where the first bishop of Virginia had been consecrated in September 1790 by the predecessor of the Archbishop of Canterbury who was with us that day. At a deep level, I am aware that the bishop of Virginia is a treasure that I hold in an earthen vessel for a time and that part of my task is to pass on that treasure undamaged to the thirteenth, fourteenth, and fifteenth bishops, and to the people whom they will serve.

Bishops also have horizontal dimensions to their ministry. Too often bishops across the centuries have so elevated their vertical sense of importance that they are not only aware of their historical significance but exaggerate it by exalting their own persons. The cathedral of the diocese of Virginia is an outdoor shrine in the Allegheny Mountains. We like to boast that our cathedral, open to the skies, has the highest roof of any cathedral in the world. It is, in a way, symbolic of the pastoral episcopate that has marked the church in Virginia for two hundred years. From 1607 until the consecration of our first bishop in 1790, the church in Virginia lived with no bishop resident, and no bishop ever visited. There were resolutions from time to time in the House of Burgesses to request Parliament to authorize a Virginia episcopate, but the resolutions never passed. Virginians viewed eighteenth-century bishops as agents of the state, overpaid and underworked aristocrats not suited for the frontier mission of a young country. When we finally consecrated our first bishop, the canons of the diocese placed severe limitations on the bishop's ministry. The diocese had no money to pay a bishop. Our first bishop was a college president; our second was a rector. What we have continued across the centuries is an itinerant episcopal ministry, a bishop on the move.

That "horizontal" episcopacy, it seems to me, is appropriate for a church with a renewed sense of the ministry of all baptized persons. The bishop is a connector and not a monarch; the bishop is one who links the diversity of gifts so that more are available for the use of all. The bishop links gifts of the people in the present with the great traditions of the past for the transformation of the future.

When a new Lutheran bishop was installed not long ago in North Dakota, he gave a list of 112 verbs to eight different assemblies across his jurisdiction with the instructions to circle 25 to 30 of the verbs that the people thought were most important for the bishop to be doing. He received 332 replies. One expects verbs such as "administer," "minister," "teach," "lead," and the like, but those came in twelfth, twenty-second, twenty-third, and twenty-fourth, respectively. The winner was "listen," followed by "encourage," "inspire," "love," and "pray."[1]

I believe a bishop who is truly at the intersection of history and at the heart of a diocese will be a listener. Such a bishop will be someone who listens to the authentic word of God across the centuries and who listens for the authentic word of this generation, discerning how those words intersect. That listening will enable the bishop to encourage, inspire, and love. It will be most acute when the bishop is a person of listening prayer.

A bishop in this model is not a new invention. The word "bishop" comes from the Greek, *episcope,* and means "oversight." It is a word which has across the centuries often had associations with both patriarchy and hierarchy. I suggest that oversight for the present and the future is simpler and more unified. The words that come to mind to amplify its meaning for our time are words like "vision," "spacious," "big picture," "inclusive," "embracing."

Part of the larger picture that we must recognize is that every generation in the church has adapted the episcopate to the circumstances of its culture and time. That has been going on from the earliest church, when the presidents of the once persecuted local Christian communities took on civic responsibilities for their cities. And just as a great river picks up soil and vegetation from every bank on its long passage to the sea, so the episcopate carries with it traces of the past far into the present and to the future.

Our purple shirts reflect the imperial role of bishops after the emperor Constantine made us officers of state. I hope we wear them with the humility and the penitence appropriate to those who repent of the oppressive use of authority. Our vestments can be derivations of the street clothes of Roman senators or convocational gowns of late medieval English parliamentarians. And our leadership styles too often echo unexamined values of cultures past and present rather than gospel values renewed for the future. Our individual pastoral letters too often use a medieval style to express a contemporary rule that sounds like a government regulation. At the other extreme, our corporate pastoral letters are too often so inclusive, so fearful of clarity, that they sound like the most tepid form of contemporary social commentary becoming quickly dated. We will always carry with us traces of the past, because we are in communion with the past. So we need to live without apology as persons who bear the past but are neither oppressed nor enamored by it. The past, and our awareness of it, can be a liberating antidote to the burdens of the present.

Bishops live at the intersection of past, present, and future, at the intersection of the vertical continuity with the history and the future of the church and the horizontal dimension of the church confronting and often embracing the concerns of the present, reaching beyond our own culture to churches across the world. Bishops who are effective at this intersection must be leaders more than managers, in touch with the multidimensional resources and demands that claim the attention of the episcopal office. Those claims change across the generations. What are the claims of our own time?

Many authors are currently commenting on how contemporary religious institutions are changing. Robert Wuthnow has written a very thoughtful book, *The Restructuring of American Religion*, in which he explores the current deemphasis on denominational identity and the rise of special purpose groups that cross denominational lines.[2] Loren Mead's *The Once and Future Church* speaks of a new paradigm as the church enters a new time in its history.[3]

Nancy Ammerman, who teaches at the Candler School of Theology in Atlanta, has commented on the American denominational future, focusing primarily on Southern Baptists.[4] Her description of Baptist experience is not unlike our own. She points out that many observers have noted that we are moving away from widely accepted patterns of what has been identified as "modern" into what are often called "post-modern" organizations. These changes are occurring in a wide variety of the institutions in our common life. A primary characteristic of a modern organization has been mass production of identical items widely distributed and sold, whether automobiles or Sunday school materials. But post-modern culture makes it possible to tailor goods and services to very particularized segments of the market. We discovered long ago in the Episcopal Church that it was not possible to mass produce a church school curriculum that would meet the needs for every congregation in every diocese across this great church of ours. Modern church organizations often had specialists at diocesan and national church levels who had highly specific functions in Christian education, social justice, and minority affairs. The staff structure of many dioceses and of our general church often continue to reflect this same specialization so characteristic of modern, corporate, organizational life. Post-modern organizations will often have generalized and multiskilled persons, Dr. Ammerman points out, much closer to the consumers and producers than large corporate bureaucracies provided.

In the Episcopal Church we are experiencing the same baby-boomer phenomenon that Baptists, Presbyterians, and so many others are experiencing, where families church-shop at the local level to find what meets their needs, or what congregations, regardless of denominational label, provide the widest range of services. It is not too hard to take issue with the consumerist mentality that fuels the church-shopping phenomenon. But it is a reality that we cannot avoid. As Dr. Ammerman summarizes, "Post-modern organizations are smaller, less centralized, less prone to over-specialization within,...less oriented to mass production and more flexible." They are, in effect, sufficiently flexible to respond to market changes. Or, to put it in biblical terms, local, flexible, listening churches are more able to tell in the tongues of local people the mighty works of God (Acts 2:12).

I believe that the episcopate is especially suited for a post-modern, dynamic, locally focused church structure. We have placed our emphasis in persons and not in systems, in gifts for ministry rather than in job descriptions. It is time to renew and reclaim those historic and yet so very contemporary aspects of ministry for the office of bishop. We are blessed, I think, to be a church that is not confined by a single confessional heritage. We are blessed to be a church that, from the long view of history, does not have very many institutional forms so entrenched that they cannot be changed. The current structure of the Executive Council and the national church dates only to the early part of this century. General Convention is just over two hundred years old, barely antique from the long view of the history of the church. What we do have that has endured, although adapted to different forms across the centuries, is the ministry of bishops, the gathering of congregations into a family called a diocese, and people gathering to proclaim the gospel of Jesus Christ, worshiping in the power of the Spirit, serving Christ by serving others.

We need to reclaim our distinctive forms of leadership so that bishops can be leaders more than managers, symbols of continuity and of change. They should be persons who gather a church in dialogue with the biblical narrative; a church constant in the apostles' teaching in the Apostles' and Nicene Creeds, enlivened through its baptismal and eucharistic experience and united by the historic episcopate, locally adapted as circumstances require.

How might those principles appear in a church of the future? We have succeeded in the Episcopal Church in affirming the ministry of all the baptized. No one seriously asserts that ministry is an exclusive function of the ordained. But we have not succeeded in declericalizing ministry. Too often, when we speak of the ministry of the laity, we mean what they do in church. I remind you of what I said at the beginning, echoing the catechism in the Book of Common Prayer: ministry means representing Christ in the world.

It is certainly vital for the laity to have their role in the governance of the church. But when we understand the bishop as a connector, as a leader at the intersection rather than as a monarch or a manager, then I think we need to release bishops for leadership. The House of Bishops should be a place where dialogue is vibrant and rich, and the House needs to be served by a small staff that helps the bishops connect with one another.

At a local, diocesan level, we have multiplied dioceses because we have expected bishops to be micromanagers of diocesan life. Of course, we have used the language of pastoral care in the multiplication of dioceses, which too often, I fear, reflects our confusion about the differences between pastoral care and therapy. A pastor can care for thousands because of the symbolic leadership of the office, and the pastor's role as teacher. A therapist has a severely limited caseload. The evidence suggests that the smaller the diocese, the more a bishop is forced to micromanage and the less available the bishop is as a pastor.

A bishop at the intersection of the life of a diocese can be served by a small staff of generalists, who help the bishop connect the people of the diocese to one another for the release of their gifts for ministry rather than performing the ministry of the diocese on behalf of the people. That vision of the episcopate enables a bishop to be a leader for a larger group because the bishop is not managing the details. Indeed, unless a diocese is sufficiently large and complex, it will lack the diversity of experiences and gifts that help people experience the universality and complexity of mission across a diverse world.

A bishop at the intersection of past, present, and future, one who stands at the intersection of the diversity of gifts and experiences in the diocese, is a bishop exercising a ministry consistent with the ordination vows in the Book of Common Prayer, consistent more with leadership than with management. What is prayed for at that sacred moment when apostolic hands are laid on the one whom the church says God has called to be a bishop? We pray that God will pour out the same princely Spirit that was present in Christ, in the apostles, and across the ages. We pray the bishop may be filled with love of God and of all people. And, in an obvious extension of that love, we pray that the bishop will feed and tend the flock. We pray that the bishop will exercise without reproach the high priesthood to which he or she is called, serving day and night in the ministry of reconciliation. That means a bishop, in the bishop's *person* far more than in his or her *job*, is a leader of reconciliation, a *pontifex*, the Latin word for high priest that also means "bridge-builder." Major intersections are bridges: across cultures, across cities, across gaps that divide people from one another. This ministry of reconciliation, the prayer of consecration goes on to say, is accomplished by declaring pardon, offering the holy gifts and wisely overseeing the life of the church. Through it all, the bishop is to lead a pure, gentle, and holy life.

There is no language here that suggests the bishop is to be a zealot, testing members of the church to see whether they conform to one or another test of orthodoxy which, like most tests for orthodoxy, are recipes for oppression. No, the emphasis is on bridge-building, nurturing, and living a life consistent with that reconciling ministry of the Christ who stretched out his arms for us on the hard wood of the cross. Yes, the bishop has a particular ministry as guardian of the faith. The prayer book requires that immediately after the laying on of hands, the bishop be delivered the Holy Scriptures. In that delivery,

the bishop is charged to feed the flock of Christ, guard and defend them in Christ's truth, and be a faithful steward. It is, I
think, a sign of the confusion of roles in the modern episcopate
that at that point in most consecration liturgies, there is a
multiplicity of presentations, each with its own elaborate language—copes, mitres, chasubles, rings, crosses, prayer books,
containers of oil, perhaps a handful of balloons or a stuffed ani-
mal with a funny face. We need to return to the centrality of
Scripture assumed by the ordination liturgy in the prayer book.

The bishop, as one who stands at the intersection of time
and history, of world and church, is to be grounded in the Holy
Scriptures. Such a leader at the intersection is not one whose
pattern of interpretation of Holy Scripture is narrow and confined by a particular time or culture. We are to guard and defend the flock of Christ in *Christ's* truth, not our own,
culturally conditioned version of that truth. A leader at the intersection where many roads converge, one who is able to have
genuine oversight and a broad view of the many roads that
come together, will help the pilgrims on those roads to respect
and understand each other, to discern the abiding unity they
share, and to see their differences as contributing to that unity.

This review of the bishop as a leader at the intersection is
faithful to Scripture, faithful to the prayer book, and consistent with the abiding themes by which Christians have understood their bishops across the ages. Translate those principles
into the next decade in the Episcopal Church and I think one
can see several emphases emerging.

First, bishops need to recover *episcope* as oversight, understood in the terms of this presentation. They need to have
broad vision, a sense of history, a broad view of the richness
and diversity of the church. They need to be grounded in Scripture but not in any one single interpretive pattern of Scripture
as if no others are useful. They need to claim their authority
and understand that authority as located at the center of the
church's life and not on top of it.

Second, a bishop needs to be more of a leader than a manager. Let our bishops be free to pray, to study, to emphasize
their particular gifts at the particular time and places to which

they are called. Let our diocesan bureaucracies be reduced and streamlined so that the energies flow to the congregations that are linked to one another through their bishop rather than being isolated from one another and too often in adversarial relationship with their bishop.

Third, separate the diversity on the agenda of a diocese from the particularity of an individual bishop's gifts. Yes, the bishop needs to respect the diversity, to understand it, to interpret that diversity across the church. But a bishop cannot be the manager of small church renewal, the developer of Sunday school curricula, the primary pastor to clergy families, the principal mission planner, and an itinerant evangelist all at the same time. The bishop is to be a leader. When we choose our bishops, let us recognize their particular gifts and honor them and play them from strength.

Fourth, let the college of bishops be free to serve the church, unencumbered by multiple committees, commissions, and legislative expectations. The episcopate is made up of persons. It is not a faceless institution but a company of colleagues, united in a common Lord, sharing a common story in Scripture and offering the holy gifts to Christ's holy people.

Bishops have served the church since the beginning. Patterns change, cultures change, and so will the ways we use our bishops. We live at a time of widespread disillusionment with leadership. The President's approval rating continues to slide. The British criticize their Royal Family. Politicians are greeted with widespread cynicism. Bankers are suspect. Doctors are sued. And what lawyer jokes have you heard today? The most celebrated leaders in our culture—if one can call them leaders—are entertainers and professional athletes, and neither are exactly the best role models for the church. So put into this context our concern for leadership in changing structures. What we expect of leadership in all sorts of institutions is changing. We have been given bishops, we believe, for the well-being and the fullness of the church. Release us for leadership at the center, at the intersection of past and present, of gospel and world, and free us to serve Christ by serving Christ's people.

Endnotes

1. Quoted in *Context*, April 15, 1993.

2. Robert Wuthnow, *The Restructuring of American Religion: Society and Faith Since World War II* (Princeton, N.J.: Princeton University Press, 1988).

3. Loren Mead, *The Once and Future Church* (Washington, D.C.: Alban Institute, 1991).

4. Nancy Ammerman, "Southern Baptists and the American Denominational Future: Organizational Implications," presented for "The American Denominational Future: The Southern Baptist Case" at the Louisville Institute for the Study of Protestantism and American Culture, March 1993.

Part Three

The Challenge of Mission and Culture

A dominant theme echoed by many speakers in the St. Louis symposium is the new climate developing in our culture. Authors as widely diverse as the Catholic Malcolm Muggeridge, the Anglican Lesslie Newbigin, and the Methodists Stanley Hauerwas and William Willimon have written of the demise of Christendom and the significance of practicing the gospel in a situation which is either hostile or indifferent. Whether in Tom Wright's description of neo-paganism in the West or in Nan Peete's statistics of the shifting racial patterns in America, the general consensus in St. Louis was that our changing cultural setting is making new demands on the mission of the church. There is a note of hope which ties each of the papers in this section together, for their question is less "what is wrong?" than "what can be done?" They share a commitment to the proclamation of the gospel, regardless of the challenges ahead.

Richard Kew has been working with global mission in one form or another for the past twenty years. Founding chairman of the South American Missionary Society, he serves today as the executive director of the Society for Promoting Christian Knowledge (SPCK/USA). He has been in the forefront of Anglican mission assistance in Russia. With Roger White, he is the author of *New Millennium, New Church*, where he brings his years of mission experience to bear directly on the current cultural situation of the Episcopal Church. Here he focuses particularly on the global mission opportunities rapidly developing in the church today, and outlines important needs for change as the church structures itself for mission.

Tom Wright is the recently installed dean of Lichfield Cathedral, formerly a fellow and chaplain of Worcester College, Oxford, and lecturer in New Testament for the University of Oxford. He has previously served as Canon Theologian of Coventry Cathedral. He is the author of numerous book,s both at the academic and popular level, including *The Climax of the Covenant, The New Testament and the People of God, Who was Jesus?* and *Bringing the Church to the World*. In his paper presented in St. Louis, Dean Wright describes the growing challenge of neo-paganism. The worship of Mammon and Eros (money and sex) which characterizes much of modern Western culture demands human sacrifice. He offers both an insightful analysis of the cultural and religious threat presented by neo-paganism and a program for the church's mission to a paganized world.

Terry Mattingly writes a nationally syndicated weekly column for the Scripps Howard News Service called "On Religion." An active Episcopal layman, he is assistant professor of communications at Milligan College in Tennessee. His paper focuses on the religious impact of popular culture, particularly the media. He argues that the church must become conversant with and address the all-pervasive messages of popular media. Mission in the future will need to be media literate.

Nan A. Peete is Canon to the Ordinary of the diocese of Atlanta. She has provided leadership in a wide range of areas in the church's life, including the General Theological Seminary, the Union of Black Episcopalians, and the board of the Episcopal Publishing Company, publisher of *The Witness*. Her essay presents the challenge of an increasingly multicultural society to the church of the future. Noting the shift in population composition, she sees a growing opportunity for mission for a church willing to adapt to the demands of inclusivity.

Nelle Bellamy recently retired as the National Archivist for the Episcopal Church. She is an adjunct professor of church history for the Episcopal Seminary of the Southwest. Her paper places the change and conflict of the church's past thirty years in the larger context of church history and looks for the means of stability in the midst of such turmoil, especially in the spirituality of Julian of Norwich. It is a vision of peace in the midst of a storm, a church which is still the church regardless of its context.

Richard Kew

The Mission Imperative: Change and Challenge

THIS IS MORE a plea than a paper, a plea that we as a church become more wise about the world and more active in it. It is a plea that we recognize how vitally important to our spiritual health and future well-being is a wholehearted commitment to global mission. For far too long the Episcopal Church, perhaps more than all other American churches, has suffered from a myopic world vision, with a reach severely limited to the local and domestic, at the expense of our global ministry and influence.

Despite the Savior's final and Great Commission to "go into all the world," the mission commitment of far too many of our congregations seems to end at the county line—if we're lucky! At best, this is shortsighted; at worst, it is disobedient. Furthermore, it reflects an anachronistic way of thinking. As a former editor of *Time* magazine has put it, "The old dividing line between foreign and domestic affairs is getting ever thinner."[1] Neither journalists, nor politicians, nor businesspersons, nor especially Christian leaders can afford to think or work in purely local or national terms.

Although Loren Mead's book *The Once and Future Church* is helpful, in many ways I believe his "think locally, not globally" stance to be strangely at odds with the emerging reality.[2] It is a truncated understanding of the mission of the church in a rapidly changing world. Today, for the first time in human history, the whole world is within the reach of a meaningful presentation of the Christian message. As uncomfortable as this truth might be to us, those who have given their lives to

Christ have been commissioned by the Holy Spirit to be witnesses to *all* humankind, across geographic and ethnic divides, as well as those who are near and dear.

As God renews the church, one of the things he seems to be doing is breathing new life into our obedience to the Great Commission to go into all the world preaching the gospel, making disciples of all nations. It is no accident that as renewal movements have deepened their footings within the Episcopal Church, a whole series of grassroots missionary initiatives have been launched. Some of these are still in their infancy, while others are reaching considerable maturity. These initiatives at their various stages of development are now challenging and altering irrevocably the way we as a church involve ourselves globally.

It is also my observation from traveling the length and breadth of this church for nearly a decade that those parishes which have little or no world vision also tend to have a diminutive, even a diminishing, understanding of the nature of local ministry. There are times when I want to shout from the housetops to my fellow Episcopalians, "Brothers, sisters, both your God and your world are far too small."

Great Changes Spawn the Greatest Opportunities

Never in our lifetime have there been greater opportunities for global ministry. A new world is literally being born before our eyes, rocking institutions, shattering great nations, and deepening spiritual hunger everywhere. Whether we like it or not, we are being dragged kicking and screaming from the tired agendas of the past, and are being forced to make a serious response to a fresh and confusing set of realities. This new world demands from us robust vision, a strong stomach, sensitivity to the leading of the Holy Spirit, the courage to experiment—even to fail—and the willingness to learn from our mistakes.

I was galvanized recently by reading the opening words of Peter Drucker's newest book, *Post-Capitalist Society*:

Every few hundred years in Western history there occurs a sharp transformation. We cross...a "divide." Within a few short decades, society rearranges itself—its world view; its basic values; its social and political structure; its arts; its institutions. Fifty years later, there is a new world. And the people born then cannot even imagine the world in which their grandparents lived and into which their own parents were born. We are currently living through just such a transformation.[3]

Unlike the past, today's transition is not limited to the Western nations; this one involves even the world's remotest corners. The modern missionary movement was born in the midst of the social and spiritual confusion of the last great chapter change in our history, the Industrial Revolution. Today we are being called to bring a different kind of missionary movement to birth all over again, this time amid radical changes that are more akin to the tumultuous events of the Renaissance and Reformation—yet instead of taking place on just one continent, this time the changes are happening on a global scale. In short order, familiar structures of world society have been shattered, while new ones have yet to coalesce. It is imperative that we in the church reshape our global ministry in light of these unprecedented international new realities.

It is a truth of apostolic history that it is at times like these that opportunities for mission and ministry are showered upon us. The greatest theology has almost always been written in the midst of *angst,* probably because these are the times *par excellence* when God challenges us to advance. Theology grows naturally out of a renewed sense of mission. Our watchword should be that old Latin tag, made popular in recent years by liberal quotation in the movie *Dead Poets' Society: Carpe Diem,* "Seize the day!"

Changed Realities

In 1919, when our church structures received their present formulation, a wholly different set of realities prevailed: the British had an empire upon which the sun never set, the

United States was flexing its muscles on the international stage, and despite a disastrous world war, the Western nations still straddled the world like huge colossi. Being guided by the Spirit and taking advantage of the political realities which then prevailed, the Western churches were busily taking the gospel to every corner of the globe as part of a great missionary movement. Those who went before us in the faith grasped that divine providence had placed them at that moment on the world stage to live out the love of Christ, and to proclaim with vigor and conviction God's truth. At that time, Western churches were the primary senders, initiators, and providers of resources. We bore upon our shoulders the ecclesiastical equivalent of "the white man's burden." Mission was from us to Africa, Asia, Latin America, the Pacific Isles, and the uttermost parts of the earth.

This picture has now changed. God has more than honored the energy and sacrifice of our forebears, and the churches they helped plant have in many places reached significant stature. Today, they are themselves becoming major senders of missionaries and resources. By 2000, there will be more missionaries working cross-culturally from Two-Thirds World churches than from all the Western churches combined. For example, the young Anglican Church in Chile is already involved in sending personnel to Spain; the diocese of Singapore has its sights set on Indonesia, while programs of theological education by extension developed in Latin America and Asia are being used in the West, as well as among the aboriginal peoples of Thailand and the newly-freed churches of the former Soviet Union.

While it is highly likely we will continue to send missionaries out from ourselves, the churches we planted, horrified by the corrosive secularity of our culture, now see the nations of the West as an increasingly fruitful mission field. In world mission, the twenty-first century is already upon us, and mission in this era onward is from everywhere to everywhere. It is also being carried out at a time when the fixed points of reference that have been our primary landmarks have either been moved, or in some cases torn down and their rubble carried away.

Third wave information technologies are now reshaping the
world. The world's economies are in confusion; new major
league players are pouring onto the field especially in Asia and
Latin America, while the governments, businesses, and educa-
tors of developed nations scramble to keep up. Within this context, an international meta-culture is being created, shaped by
a thousand different influences. Chief among them are Hollywood, the mass media, music, and popular culture. The vehicle
most often used is the English language. All are advancing
secular Western values, thought, and behavior patterns. One
critic states:

> Western culture is now becoming the culture of all peoples, but
> it is increasingly sick—and the whole bit is being exported, in-
> cluding our social problems, to the whole world. And so we
> must solve this for the sake of the whole world.[4]

Meanwhile, just as secularism's reach becomes universal and
seems to have almost unlimited resources to further its cause,
the axe is being laid to the trunk of its tree. The collapse of
communism has been a terrible blow to the credibility of the
secularist, materialistic way of managing a community. Anyone who has been to Russia and Eastern Europe in the last few
years knows that folks there, as they earnestly ponder the future, are anxious for the health of their souls. Parts of the Is-
lamic world are already in revolt against what they consider to
be the perniciousness of Western, secular ways. In addition,
the leaders of Islam have a far-reaching evangelistic strategy to
bring the world under the obedience of the Prophet. Hinduism
is becoming an increasingly militant force spilling outward
from India. Closer to home, the fascination with New Age su-
perstition in the West demonstrates the deep yearnings in
secularized souls that our consumer society can never satisfy.

George Weigel tells us that "the unsecularization of the
world is one of the dominant social facts of life in the late
twentieth century."[5] It is against such a background, pregnant
with opportunities, that we are called and commissioned to
bring the gospel to a hurting and needy world. The Master's

Great Commission is as relevant now as it was when he initially sent out his followers to "make disciples of all nations."

Effective Alternatives

With the best will in the world, centralized structures of mission find it extremely hard to handle such fast-changing diversity. Any attempts to do so will destroy initiative, miss opportunities, and worse still, cramp the Holy Spirit's style. Like Paul, we need at a moment's notice to be able to scrap old plans, make new ones, and respond to insistent calls to "come over to Macedonia" (Acts 16:9). Today's mission agency has to be a fast-responding operation, well-managed and able to turn on a dime. We cannot afford the luxury of being locked in by triennial budgets, ponderous resolutions of General Convention, and bureaucratic structures. I am increasingly convinced that those grassroots initiatives—the voluntary, independent mission agencies which we have already mentioned—are the best enablers for mission that the church has, and that they have been raised up by God for just such a time as this.

As sodalities focused on one or two particular tasks, mission societies enable us to make a realistic response to global challenges, be entrepreneurial in mission, and strive after excellence in a particular field. While honoring our church's received structures but not having hands tied by them, independent agencies are able swiftly to address new challenges and fresh opportunities, which in today's world arise with startling velocity. During the last year, for example, we at SPCK have been able to make a significant course change, moving from a mild interest but no involvement in Russia into three crucial education and publishing ministries, in cooperation with the Orthodox Church and in a network with dioceses and parishes here at home. While I still think we have been too slow, most other structures would have found it difficult to reorder priorities to meet such a strategic challenge so quickly.

In addition, independent societies provide the grassroots with ownership of mission, as well as being directly accountable to those who entrust resources to them. A centralized structure is not designed to function in this way. If we in the societies mismanage our mission or fail to keep our supporters informed, not only are we committing organizational suicide, we are also failing to advance the kingdom of God. This means we cannot afford to just *do* the work, we must be in constant dialogue with our constituencies, responding to their questions and curiosity, *educating* them to understand, pray for, and be part of our work. In short, we must always be working hard to make them part of our family.

Independent mission agencies also seem better able to relate to interdenominational and transdenominational specialist agencies, which are increasingly important players in global ministry. These include well-known Western agencies like Wycliffe Bible Translators and World Vision, both of which have strong Episcopal involvement, as well as emerging Two-Thirds World organizations who have committed themselves to specific tasks, such as the evangelization of India's villages or the production of literature in Latin America.

In addition, a polity of independent societies leaves room for the formation of new agencies which can be established as new areas of need are identified. In this kind of environment, those who have outlived their usefulness find it easier to go out of existence without upsetting the whole world missions applecart. My organization, SPCK/USA, was brought into being because a group of Episcopalians recognized the need for an agency to undertake certain facets of the information task for world mission. More recently, Anglican Frontier Missions has been founded because the missionary task is far from over; there are a number of groups all over the world where there has yet to be planted a viable witnessing church. Yes, despite arguments to the contrary, there is still a need for missionaries, but they are likely to work and be supported in very different ways than we have been used to.

In April this year I spent an afternoon with one of our diocesan bishops talking about the missionary needs of the United States. Perhaps the time has come, he ruminated, to form a home missionary society that will deliberately set out to establish Episcopal congregations that can reach some of the mil-

lions of unchurched people in this country. This is still an idea
and a dream, but I for one, would love to see it become a reality, because we as a church are particularly well positioned to
reach this strategic target population.

Whole World Partnerships

Networks of partnerships have to be the missionary style for
our times, both within and beyond our own denominational
allegiance. Within the Episcopal Church this has already begun. Several years ago the voluntary agencies and national
church organizations formed themselves into a cooperative
network, the Episcopal Council for Global Mission, which is
starting to make itself felt. But the kind of partnership about
which I am talking goes far beyond this.

In the future, partnerships will of necessity cross confessional boundaries, and will involve ties with interdenominational entities that are surging into existence in South Korea,
Argentina, and Tanzania, to name only a few countries. We
have much to share within these new relationships, but we
also have a tremendous amount to learn. In many of these networks, we in the Western churches will not be the Lone Rang-
ers on our white horses, armed with silver bullets. Instead, we
will be the Tontos, providing support and help to Two-Thirds
World agencies when asked. This will require unprecedented
humility on our part. Pray God we have the grace to recognize
this and warm to it.

The Episcopal Council for Global Mission is at the front end
of a reshaping of the church's structure for more effective
global involvement, but we have a long way to go. The voluntary agencies, working cooperatively with the Partnerships
Unit of the national church, seem set to continue their advance and will keep asking the difficult questions about how
world mission should be undertaken in an uncertain future. It
is clear to *all* of us involved in world mission that the time has
come to significantly rethink and rework the way we do our
business.

As a starting point for discussion, I want to make the following suggestion. In preparation for this symposium I have consulted as many as possible who are involved in global ministry, who have given me their input for this paper. Thus this suggestion is not mine alone, but reflects the feelings of many in the Episcopal world mission community. I believe the Partnerships Officer is a crucial position on the Presiding Bishop's staff. However, rather than managing a huge department with oversight of the whole global task, this executive should be akin to the Secretary of State for the Episcopal Church. The officer and a small staff ought to handle interchurch, inter-Anglican, international relationships for our province of the Anglican Communion. Beyond that, the Partnerships Officer should work with the independent agencies and other mission entities as we respond to emerging realities. But rather than managing the doing of the work, the task of the Partnerships Officer should be to provide information, research, and services for the agencies.

There are certain tasks voluntary societies should not be asked to do, and which they should not attempt to do. It is my observation that the Church of England has not been served well by its voluntary agencies when it has asked them to undertake the diplomatic side of global ministry. On the other hand, in Britain, where independent agencies have always predominated, there has been a long history of missionary innovation, as well as that necessary responsiveness to the grassroots which our inherited system lacks.

Not only does a Partnerships Officer as "Secretary of State" keep the diplomatic side of the global task firmly in the Presiding Bishop's bailiwick, where it truly belongs, it also frees the agencies to do their job without too many distractions. By reducing or even eliminating the direct conduct of mission by the national church, the Partnerships Officer and a small staff have a much clearer and much more "do-able" role. Also, if most of the conduct of mission is in the hands of the voluntary agencies, the Partnerships Officer will of necessity have to develop an intimate relationship with the societies, and as a result will be kept in touch with the ever-changing challenge of global ministry, as well as the responsiveness of the grassroots.

Structures for Mission

How we structure the church to be faithful in its global ministry is only a small part of the whole story, for it is the Spirit of God who inspires the People of God to tell the tale of sins forgiven, through the sacrificial love of our Lord Jesus Christ. God does not function unilaterally; he uses us as his agents and mouthpieces. A major task before those of us who are committed to the spread of the gospel to the ends of the earth is to educate and persuade our fellow Episcopalians not only that this is a worthwhile commitment, but that this is an unavoidable obedience, and that our own future health depends upon it.

As excited as I am about the potential for change arising out of this fine symposium, it troubles me that, despite the fact that the globe appears prominently on the logo of the gathering, this is the only session in which we are considering the Episcopal Church's responsibility in reaching the whole world with the gospel. I fear this reflects the ongoing low priority given to global witness in our tradition in the United States, and demonstrates what a long way we still have yet to go. I press it so hard because "mission is both a means of transformation and a means of being transformed."[6]

Church structures in the future, however the pieces finally come together, have to be *mission* structures. Our primary focus has to be upon those outside the walls of our comfortable, and sometimes rather smug, little churches. Whether they be our secular neighbors in suburbia who shrug their shoulders and say "I don't know what you are talking about" when we mention God and the way Jesus Christ gives meaning to our lives, indigenous peoples in the Amazon rain forests, the teeming millions of Calcutta's slums, or sophisticated businesspersons in Hong Kong, Tokyo, or Istanbul, their welfare and relationship with God must be our priority. In the past, we have either spent too much time on tasks which are peripheral to gospel proclamation, or have been caught up in what Sam Shoemaker called our "little round of pious duties." These are luxuries we can no longer afford in an increasingly hostile world. It is my dream that within the next generation every congregation of this wonderful church of ours will catch the vision; that they will become actively involved in cross-cultural, international ministry, reaching out to "bring good news to the poor...to proclaim release to the captives and recovery of sight to the blind, to let the oppressed go free, to proclaim the year of the Lord's favor" (Luke 4:18-19).

Endnotes

1. Henry A. Grunwald, "The Post-Cold War Press: A New World Needs New Journalism," *Foreign Affairs* (Summer 1993), p. 15.

2. Loren Mead, *The Once and Future Church* (Washington, D.C.: Alban Institute, 1991).

3. Peter F. Drucker, *Post-Capitalist Society* (New York: Harper Business, 1993), p. 1.

4. Harold Turner is quoted by George G. Hunter III in *How to Reach Secular People* (Nashville: Abingdon, 1992), p. 25.

5. George Weigel is quoted by Samuel P. Huntingdon in "The Clash of Civilizations," *Foreign Affairs* (Summer 1993), p. 26.

6. Bruce Larson is quoted by George G. Hunter III in *How to Reach Secular People,* p. 117.

Tom Wright

The New Paganisms

AS YOU WALK through an airport in the Western world, you receive all kinds of revealing cultural messages. I want to begin by highlighting three of them. My task in this paper is to give you a glimpse of some aspects of contemporary paganism, and then to suggest what we should be doing about it. I don't know what the word "paganism" suggests to you; until recently its only reference point in Britain was to the old religion that preceded Christianity, and whose only current representatives were a few flaky groups huddled around Stonehenge on midsummer morning. Well, that sort of paganism is back in business today with a vengeance, and I shall come to it presently. But I want to start in the airport, with the signs of the times that tell me we are already deep into a different sort of paganism. Consider these three messages one by one.

First, there is the Visa advertisement. It makes use of the intertwined rings of the Olympic logo, and its slogan is breathtakingly simple: "Visa makes the world go round." Now I think that's actually blasphemous. A generation ago one might have heard smoochy songs saying, "Love makes the world go round." The Beatles broke the mold by singing, "Money don't get everything, it's true; what it don't get, I can't use"; now, in line with Madonna and her "Material Girl" philosophy, we have Visa quite baldly stating a creed by which billions live without even thinking about it. As long as it was love, one could pull it vaguely toward Christianity: love, if you read it the right way, might turn out to be a synonym for God, or so we could comfort ourselves with thinking. But Visa? Visa can only be the messenger of a god, and the god is of course Mammon.

The reason the false gods are powerful is that, as they've been doing ever since the garden of Eden, they offer you the chance to play at being God yourself. So it is with the second sign of the times. The Mastercard advertisement has the two globes of the Mastercard logo held by two hands in what used to be a praying position, and the slogan this time comes straight out of Genesis 3: "You've got the whole world in your hands." Now again that comes out of an old song, but who was it who had the whole world in his hands? God, of course. "Just eat this," said the serpent, "and you will be like gods, knowing good and evil." "Just use this card," says the advertisement, "and you will be like gods, knowing credit and debit." You will have arrived. Those who worship at the shrine of Mammon are assured of an inflated sense of their own humanness. They get to own the world. Jesus told a parable about someone who thought like that, and the word "fool" occurred prominently in its punchline. That, of course, is what the advertisements don't say.

Now don't get me wrong. I am not saying that credit cards are themselves diabolical. I shall come to further analysis and suggestions of ways forward presently; at the moment I just want you to notice that some of our most prestigious companies, whom we may safely assume hired advertising agencies who knew their business, decided to hook into a paganized version of certain bits of post-Christian folk-religion which could be taken over smoothly, gently, so that people would hardly notice.

So Mammon is making his presence felt in our contemporary culture—not of course for the first time, but in new and quite startling ways. But Mammon isn't the only god on the block today. What about Aphrodite, or Venus, the goddess of erotic love? I don't need to tell you that we are surrounded, bombarded, with the message that if we worship at her shrine our lives will gain a new dimension, will find new levels of excitement and deep personal enrichment. And I don't need to tell you either—at least, I don't need to tell those of you who, like me, work in a pastoral ministry—that hidden under the gloss there, too, is the word "fool." More than half of the people I counsel come to me in despair because someone, either themselves or somebody else, has believed Aphrodite's spurious claim and tried to live by it. They have burned brightly for a while, like an electric lightbulb with too many volts going through it, and then there has been a great explosion, a bad smell, and darkness. And for those who live in the darkness it is hard to see anything at all, except, so Aphrodite whispers, by finding another lightbulb and running a million volts through it this time.

And in the airports we are again confronted with startling signs of these new pagan times. "Don't leave home without it" was quite a friendly and innocuous way of advertising the American Express card. Now similar phrases advertise condoms. "Going far?" the advertisement inquires of the traveler, with the kind of double-entendre one might expect from a tipsy stranger in a pub. The message is clear: of course we assume you'll be having lots of casual sex, but please be sensible, because we don't want any nasty diseases, do we? Again, don't get me wrong. I'm not a dualist: I know from Scripture and from experience that sex is one of God's wonderful gifts. But Aphrodite has lied her way to the heart of our Western culture with the news that life without genital sexual relations is not worth living. It does not downgrade the Creator's wonderful gift of sexuality to say that this is a straightforward, pagan lie.

My fourth sign of the times comes not from the airport, but from a parking lot. It concerns another contemporary manifestation of paganism, most evident within our culture, though I think more blatantly so in yours than in mine. At a conference recently in another part of the United States, I drove up behind a car that had three bumper-stickers, ranging from one with large letters to one with small letters. As I got closer I saw them in turn, and this was how I reacted.

The first one said, boldly: "CHINA HAS GUN CONTROL." Being a stranger, I didn't get the point at once. Could it be saying that, since China was so much more backward than we were, if even *they* had gun control then surely we should as well? The second sign, as it came into view, told me that this reading was mistaken. Whatever China does, the message was saying, is the opposite of the right way to do things. The second sign said: "A MAN WITH A GUN IS A CITIZEN. A MAN WITHOUT A GUN IS A SUBJECT." This was pretty clear. But I wasn't at all prepared, then, for the third sign, which in its smaller print seemed to me to sit extremely awkwardly, almost like a sad little protest, over against the other two. It said: "Life is fragile; handle with prayer."

All right, there are complex cultural and other issues involved here. This is simply how it strikes me: our culture has worshiped at the shrine of another great pagan god, the god Mars, the ancient and now the very modern god of war. We have done it on a large scale. Without at all condoning the actions of certain other countries, I observe as a historian that the Western world has always needed, ever since Roman times at least, to demonize its neighbors a little further to the East, and that we have been doing that just as much in recent days as we ever did in the days of Jesus. And we have also done it on a small scale: whatever the rights and wrongs of individuals carrying small arms in a pioneer society, we now live in a world where personal violence, often gratuitous, has become a way of life for many, and hence a way of death for many. And I don't think it takes much prophetic insight to state that this was not how the Creator intended the world to be.

Paganisms of the Left and Right

What preliminary conclusions can we draw from these examples, these signs of the times, about the nature of contemporary or any other paganism? Three things. First, paganism elevates and worships some part of God's good creation, changing it from being a good thing to being a god, which it never was. Second, in doing so it offers, and delivers for a short time if you're lucky, an inflated sense of your own humanness. It feels extra good to be alive. Paganism is a drug: worshiping the god gives you a shot in the arm. Third, however, paganism demands sacrifices. Sometimes the sacrifices are human ones; regularly they include certain vital parts of one's own humanity. Serious paganism is extremely bad for you and for those whose lives are enmeshed with yours, but that doesn't stop it from being attractive.

These paganisms, especially Mammon and Mars, can be loosely called paganisms of the right. They are part of our modern materialistic society, and tend to hunt together. Part of the reason for Mars-worship in the modern world is that the makers of weapons are in business to serve Mammon, not their fellow human beings. The pornography and related industries are doing what they're doing in the service of Mammon, too; without that, many of the exploited women and children in the world would be left alone. And Mars leads to Aphrodite; the stress of war and violence leaves those involved, both directly and indirectly, with huge emotional wounds and scars, with needs and urges which only a large binge of Aphrodite-worship seems able to satisfy. And so the wheel of paganism goes round, crushing under its uncaring weight millions of children, women, and men every year.

And there are those within the church who dare not lift a finger against paganism lest they be accused of dualism, of rejecting the proper use of money, the good and joyful experience of healthy sexuality, and the necessity of security in a brutal world where lunatics go armed to the teeth. How are we to find our way through this nightmare? And how can we rethink and reshape the life of our church so as to address these issues properly?

Before we get to that, let me turn to what we may loosely call paganisms of the left. You don't need me to tell you that the New Age movements have been on the increase of late and have gained a considerable following all across the Western world, not least in some of the churches. What I want to point out to you is how we got there. In the eighteenth-century Enlightenment, God was banished upstairs. Even saying the word God with a capital "G" seems to conjure up an image (within our culture at least) of a rather distant and remote figure, "way beyond the blue" as the hymn says. Our culture bought heavily into Deism, with its distant and detached God, so unlike the passionate and involved God we find in Scripture. A good deal of Christian theology in the last two hundred years has been written as though this view of things were true, so that we find it hard to break out of the Deist mold.

But what happened next was perhaps predictable. If you make God simply a landlord, a remote figure vaguely responsible for the world but not intimately involved with it, he soon becomes an absentee landlord. God is so remote that we have to get on and run the world ourselves; religion then becomes escapism. But from there it's just a short step to atheism: the absentee landlord becomes simply an absentee. And the post-Deist atheism is only a halfway house to rediscovering other gods. When you kiss goodbye to the old man in the sky, you find the old lady of the earth waiting to greet you instead. For some, this means a move toward Eastern religions; for others, a voyage of self-discovery and sexual exploration.

This search for a new god is why the New Age movements have become so popular of late, because humans beings are not naturally atheists. Robbed of one god, we will find another elsewhere. The New Age offers a classic pagan solution: the world itself is divine. Don't look for a god outside the world; find one within, within the earth, the soil, the blood, the loins, the dark forces that can be unleashed if you summon them up from within. Ultimately, as Matthew Fox claims in some of his writings, we discover that we ourselves are divine. This, I suggest, despite its apparently Christian language, is simply another sort of paganism. Just as Deism produces a parody of the biblical doctrine of God's transcendence, so the New Age produces, by reaction, a parody of the biblical doctrine of God's immanence.

This sort of serious neo-paganism, of course, doesn't stop there. Once you take a step down the road of saying that the earth is divine (perhaps calling it "Gaia," which can reflect a serious scientific hypothesis but can also reflect a serious paganism), you put yourself in the way of all kinds of disturbing phenomena. The rise of modern witchcraft is a serious and deeply disturbing trend within our culture; what used to be the private world of a few has become the increasingly public world of increasingly large numbers. There is of course a danger of paranoia, of seeing demons behind every bush. But the sober, serious evidence suggests that in my country, and I think in yours, the invoking of dark and destructive powers has taken on a new life in recent years. The paganism of the left, no less than the paganism of the right, is back in serious business.

Once again, there are those in the churches who see all this and don't even think anything is the matter. In my own country we have seen New Age-style ceremonies in some of our major cathedrals. Some Christians are so anxious to avoid the suggestion of dualism—of rejecting the material world as though it were trash, or of exploiting it as though we could rape it with impunity—that they have welcomed any and all alternatives as though they were equally valuable. That is shallow and foolish. Of course we must respect and value the good world which our God has made. Of course we must find ways forward to serious ecological responsibility. But we won't do that if we treat the world simply as divine. We must hammer out ways forward that do justice to theological truth, and hence to every aspect of reality, not simply engage in knee-jerk reactions this way or that.

One particular way in which this move toward paganism is manifesting itself can be seen in my own field, that of the study of the New Testament. There is a serious move afoot today, spearheaded by the so-called Jesus Seminar and particularly by such scholars as Burton Mack and Ron Cameron, to de-Judaize the gospel tradition, and to make Jesus and the early Christians basically a variety of pagan philosophers whose mission was not to announce the kingdom but to tease people into "living with verve" in a difficult and tumultuous time. I don't want to discuss this in any detail here, but just to note that one reason why such ideas are gaining currency today, for all their utter historical implausibility, is that they fit with the prevailing mood. The Jesus Seminar's Jesus is on the way to being a New Age Jesus, leaving Jesus the Jew and Jesus the crucified and risen Messiah out of the picture altogether. As a historian and theologian, one of my major tasks is to combat such suggestions; for today's purpose, I simply note where it fits into the current scene.

Confronting Paganism with the Gospel

One of the most comforting things about recognizing that we are facing serious paganism on all sides is that it puts us firmly on the map of early Christianity. Paul was the apostle to the gentiles, the pagans. We tend to forget this by overemphasizing the debates he had with his own Jewish tradition, but it is time to reemphasize it, as he does himself in letter after letter. The early church was surrounded by paganism and addressed its gospel to the pagan world, saying that there was a god who was different from the gods traditionally worshiped, a god who was the creator of all and so not to be confined within aspects of the world—and at the same time a god who was closer than breath itself and whose image could be glimpsed, as in a distorting mirror, in fallen humankind. This god, the god of the Jews (that was always a hard thing for the pagans to swallow, and it has remained so), had now fully and savingly revealed himself in Jesus, the Jewish Messiah, and in his death and resurrection; and this god now offered his own spirit to those who would worship him, to enable them to bear his image truly in his world, and so to be the agents of his coming kingdom.

One vital aspect of biblical theology that is often ignored must be stressed at this point. It is clear in the Old Testament that the answer of the true God to the problem of evil is to establish his covenant with Israel. Let me spell that out a bit. The problem of evil is, basically, the problem of paganism, in which humans worship that which is not God and so distort both their own humanness and the world to which they should be reflecting the true God. God's answer to this problem is to work from within, to call a family of sinful human beings to be the light of the world, the means of replacing curse with blessing. The gospel of Jesus claims that this plan, this covenant plan, has reached its great climax: evil has been decisively defeated in Jesus' death, God's new world has been decisively inaugurated in Jesus' resurrection, and God's new people—the followers of Jesus—are equipped with God's own Spirit to be the means of implementing that victory and that new creation, bringing the healing and loving rule of God to bear upon the world which still labors and groans under the weight of paganism.

Recognizing that we are faced with choices similar to those of the early Christians ought to help us see how this gospel can be distorted. When the church faces paganism it is always tempted to go in one of two directions. The power of paganism tempts you either to assimilate or to escape, either to embrace a form of paganism—even if you continue to use Christian language for a time—or to retreat into dualism, into a rejection of the world altogether. We can see how the early church struggled with these alternatives. Some tried to put together a package that was basically three parts paganism and one part Christianity. That is how some people today understand the Constantinian settlement; I'm not sure that does justice to what was actually going on, but perhaps you see the point. Others tried a philosophy that was basically dualistic: the world is a snare and a delusion, and true spirituality consists in escaping from it into a sphere of private religion. Hence, gnosticism. The church later held together two modes of being Christian in uneasy tension: the papacy and the monastic movement, those (in Henry Chadwick's memorable phrase) who sought to rule the world and those who sought to renounce it. But the tension always points to a different solution, which the assimilator and the dualist both miss. The church is called to redeem the world.

How? I now want to make some suggestions about how today we can and must combat the serious neo-paganisms of both right and left, and how the church can be geared so that our structures support this vocation rather than work against it. It seems to me that we are living today at a moment when the church, having increasingly lived and preached a dualistic message, is suddenly realizing the danger of dualism and is wondering what to do. In that context, voices all around the church tell us that we must, in effect, assimilate to the world. We must resonate with it, sympathize with it, share its life, do its thing. A good deal of the pressure within the Episcopal Church today comes, I believe, at exactly this point. Holiness is forgotten in the quest for a wholeness that is finding divinity within itself. Old moral standards are rejected as dualistic, as anti-creation. I believe we must oppose this shallow assimilationism, but I believe we must oppose it without lapsing back into the dualism that it has rightly rejected.

One of the most striking things that the early Christians did can be seen in their building of churches. If you go to an archaeological site in Britain where they have dug up Roman remains, you will again and again see the remains of a Christian church, built on top of a pagan shrine to Mithras or some other god. What were they up to? Was that not somewhat tactless toward their pagan neighbors, toward the representatives of older native religions in Britain and elsewhere? Alternatively, was there not a danger of compromise, of transferring to Jesus aspects of religious worship that belonged to the old pagan gods?

It may have been tactless and there was a danger of compromise, but I suggest that the basic instinct was totally sound. To build elsewhere implies at once that Jesus is simply one revelation among others, or that the God whom the church worships is simply one god among others. To put up a new building at a safe distance down the road fits with the prevailing cultural mood of the Enlightenment, and it has left us today with churches that are literally and metaphorically down the road, at a safe distance from the places where serious pagan worship is being offered. Those who are trying to subvert Christianity with New Age worship know better. They aren't satisfied with celebrating neo-paganism in private; they want to do it in cathedrals, to take over Christianity on its own turf.

The thing to grasp is that paganism, properly understood, is a parody of the truth. God made a beautiful world; paganism lures you to worship it. God made a world of enormous power and potential; paganism entices you to harness that power for your own benefit, whether through Mars, Mammon, Aphrodite, Gaia, or straightforward witchcraft. We gain nothing by ignoring the truth about God's world, and retreating into a private sphere. We must take the risk, and find ways today of worshiping the true God on ground at present occupied by the pagan gods and goddesses. We must reclaim the world for the God to whom it belongs. The gospel is not about escaping from the world, but about the true God healing the world. And healing comes about through the people of this God worshiping him truly, and thereby being equipped to bear his image—his healing, restoring image—to shine with his light within the world.

So what might it mean, today, to worship the God revealed in Jesus on turf presently occupied by pagan idols? Let's take them one by one. We must dethrone Mammon from his all-powerful position in our society. Giving money away in the name of Christ is a vital and powerful symbolic action. Choosing poverty in the name of Christ is folly to those who worship Mammon, but in every generation God calls some to do it as a sign that Mammon is not after all the true God. Credit cards are a convenience, but we must find ways to prevent them from sustaining their grandiose and even blasphemous claims. Giving up using them for Lent might be a start. And, at the macro-level, we must find ways of addressing the major economic problems of our world from a Christian perspective. The world is hungry, literally, for a new economic order. Producing it might mean the rich nations taking a serious cut in living standards for a while. Anyone who follows Jesus knows that a price like that is precisely what we should expect: he was rich beyond all splendor, but all for love's sake became poor. Do we have the will, for ourselves, for our churches, and for our communities, to make hard decisions in the name of Christ?

What about Mars? One of the problems in our world today is that our old stories have let us down. The West used to say that if only we got rid of communism, the world would be fine. Then it happened, and it still isn't fine. We don't know what to do about Bosnia or Somalia because our world-view didn't allow for things like this. We had forgotten that communism was not the real evil, that the real evil lay in the hearts and wills of human beings no matter what system they lived under. So our machines of war, which were geared to fighting great ideological enemies, are ill-equipped for the more serious task of policing a dangerous world, of preventing the arrogant and powerful from trampling upon the weak. We desperately need to do for the world as a whole what civilized nations did for themselves a long while back: to provide a police force that will protect the lives and the rights of the innocent, and will do so with full public support because its actions are seen to be just. This is the truth of which Mars-worship is the parody: that the God who made the world desires order and justice, desires the weak to be protected against predators, desires to see his image reflected in his human creatures, not defaced and battered. The sign that we are giving up Mars-worship and worshiping Jesus instead will be that we, as nations and as churches, find ways of addressing these problems which may be costly but which will result in real justice and not papering over cracks.

As for Aphrodite, it is surely clear to all of us that we aren't going to get anywhere by marginalizing our sexuality, even if that were possible in today's world. At the same time, we must celebrate the vocation to celibacy as a good and God-given possibility, and affirm celibates in that vocation without constantly implying, as our society does in a million ways today, that life without genital sexual activity is a serious handicap. But we must also celebrate Christian marriage, and find ways of doing so which are creative, not merely to preserve old "family values," which of course vary enormously from culture to culture, but to show that God's gift of sexuality is such a rich and precious thing that it's worth putting in its proper context. There are those today, in the church as well as outside it, who are so obsessed with sexuality that they can think of little else. Any attempt to set clear moral standards is seen as an affront to the goddess they are implicitly worshiping. This nonsense must be named for what it is, and, instead, we must learn to glorify God with our bodies, learning afresh the joy and the beauty and the God-givenness of chastity. I hardly need add that several major social problems would look very different if that message were to be taken seriously. Did the creator God really intend his children to be dependent upon a rubber sheath for their happiness and well-being?

When it comes to Gaia, it is again surely clear by now that we must be committed in the name of Jesus to serious ecology. We know from Paul's letter to Rome that the whole creation is groaning in travail, and we ourselves groan with it. It is no part of Christian discipleship to treat the world as either a private gold mine or a private garbage dump on the grounds that God is going to throw it in the trash quite soon anyway. That is not the teaching of Scripture. God is going to renew the whole world: new heavens and a new earth is what we're promised, and the great act by which God will do this began with the resurrection of Jesus from the dead on Easter Day. To imply that the created order is to be thrown away, after which God will do something quite different, reflects a theology that would leave Jesus rotting in the tomb, while the church worships a Christ of faith on a quite different plane of reality. If that fact were fully grasped, we would see less ecological irresponsibility among fundamentalists for whom the bodily resurrection of Jesus has been a doctrinal shibboleth cut off from its true significance. And if that fact were grasped elsewhere in the church, we would see an ecological responsibility that owed nothing to the New Age movements or to Gaia-worship. We are to be healing stewards of creation, not because creation is divine, but because God is God, and wills his human creatures to reflect his image to the world.

In these and many, many other ways we are called, I believe, in this new generation, at a moment of great cultural crisis, to worship the true God on territory at present claimed, wrongly, by false gods. The whole earth is full of the glory of the true God. We as Christians are called to celebrate that. In and through all of this we are called, I believe, to a serious recapturing of the vision of God as Trinity. That doctrine, which for two hundred years has been mocked as a piece of patristic perplexity by semi-Deists who didn't believe we could know anything about God very clearly, is coming back into its own, as we might expect. It was, after all, hammered out not as a piece of abstract speculation but as the lifeblood of a church facing paganism at every level. As we find ourselves in a similar position, we need to rediscover the joy of Trinitarian theology, as necessary mental equipment with which to think through the major issues we face, and as necessary spiritual equipment if we are to worship the true God and so resist the blandishments of the false ones.

Paganisms and the Structures of the Church

There is much more that I could say. I have said nothing about spiritual warfare, though that is a vital part of the whole picture. I have said nothing about the renewals with which God has been equipping his church to face the new challenges, the new movements of all sorts. Those (not least in the media) who want to stick with the categories of the fifties and sixties—evangelical, liberal, catholic, and so on—are increasingly outdated. But I want to conclude with a reflection on the implications of what I've been saying for the theme of this conference as a whole.

First, the church must be shaped as the community that worships the true God. This is not something we can take for granted. It is not just a matter of going on saying the daily offices and hoping all will be well—though let me say that the trivializing of liturgy on the one hand, and the abandonment of it on the other, which are currently taking place in some Anglican and Episcopal circles, are a recipe for human-centered worship in the short term and disaster for our mission in the long term. No, we must re-grasp the holistic vision of Paul in Romans 12: our whole lives, our whole lives as a church, are to be an act of worship of the true triune God, and our structures must reflect that.

Second, our styles of leadership must reflect the God whom we worship. If at the moment leadership has been in danger of becoming management, and management in danger of becoming dictatorship, this can only be because we are implicitly worshiping a god other than the one revealed in the Servant King. Ironically, the business world has recently been learning fast that its old bullying styles of management aren't nearly as good as a caring, humanizing model—just at the moment when the church has increasingly been copying old business styles in its dress, its offices, and (alas) in its bullying and emotional blackmail. The irony is double, because contemporary management studies have as their bottom line the continuing worship of Mammon: now, we are told, you will make more money if you care for your employees properly! The church must be in the vanguard of those who are doing the right thing, but for the right reason. We must rethink our structures so as to reflect true belief in the true God: the creating Father, the servant Son, and the energizing Spirit.

Third, the church must expect to be the suffering community, the place where the pain of the world is experienced in the presence of God. Christians aren't called to be apart from the pain of the world. Romans 8 holds out a model of the world groaning, then of Christians groaning within the world, and then of the Spirit groaning within Christians. The church is to be the place where the groaning of the world is held within the love of God. Therefore we must not be surprised when the pain of the church, for instance at the moment on issues of sexuality and gender, reflects the pain of the world. This doesn't mean we have got it all wrong, that we have taken a wrong turn somewhere. It means that we are being called to resonate with the pain of the world, and to bring that pain, as Christ did, into the very presence of God, so that it may be healed. The church, like Christ, is of course called to remain holy as this process takes effect. But we must not be surprised, or angry with one another, as we find this pain in our midst. That is part of the whole process of being the church for the world, of confronting paganism in its pain with the flesh-and-blood fact of the love of God in Christ and by the Spirit.

Fourth and finally, as we go about exploring the tasks which God has for us to do in combatting neo-paganism, we are to do so with joy. In my New Testament studies recently I have been struck by the fact that in first-century Judaism we find a people looking forward eagerly to something that their God is going to do for them, and in first-century Christianity we find a people, with more or less exactly the same world-view, looking back to something that their God has just done, climactically, in the middle of history, by which everything has been changed, by which a new world has been inaugurated. Nothing else than the resurrection will explain this change historically, and it was the resurrection of Jesus that drove those early disciples out to confront the paganism of their world with the good news that the true God of the world had acted in love and power to rescue his world and his people from their bondage.

We go to our tasks, then, not gloomily, as though we were simply to criticize everyone else and grumble about the terrible state of the world. We go with joy, knowing that the pagan parody is nothing compared with the real truth, that pagan pleasure has nothing to match Christian joy. As we together, on both sides of the Atlantic and indeed around the world, reshape our future as Christians and as Anglicans or Episcopalians, we must take care that our structures and our practices are shot through with joy. We believe in the God who makes the world go round, in the God who has the whole world in his hands. We believe this because of Jesus and the Spirit. And this, if we are truly grasped by it, will give us a joy that makes our mission radically different from all others. Don't leave home without it.

Terry Mattingly

And Now a Word From Your Culture

TRUE OR FALSE: It is impossible to talk in terms of practical details and statistics about how modern Americans live their
lives without addressing the role played by television and other
forms of news and entertainment media.

True or false: Most churches have little or nothing practical
to say about the role that television and other forms of news
and entertainment media play in the daily lives of most modern Americans.

True or false: Most churches have little or nothing practical
to say about the daily lives of most modern Americans.

True or false: This applies to my church.

Let me stress that, by asking these questions, I am not suggesting that Christian theology and church traditions are irrelevant. I do, however, want to force church leaders to talk
about the statistical realities of life in modern America: dollars,
cents, hours, pocket calendars, wallets, and free time. Our goal
is to think in secular terms, for a few moments.

Beyond any shadow of doubt, the answer to questions one
and two is "true." As a religion columnist and Christian educa-
tor, I am convinced that the answer to the third question is
also "true." I will leave the answer to question four up to you.

A few years ago I wrote an article for the *Rocky Mountain
News* about the Jewish holiday of *Sukkot,* an autumnal celebration that many of us would know from biblical references to
the Feast of Tabernacles. In order to learn more about *Sukkot,* I
visited the home of an Orthodox rabbi in Denver and we sat in
the tabernacle that he had built in his backyard. As we dis-

cussed various traditions and scriptures, the rabbi's teenaged sons joined us. Obviously, the teenaged sons of an ultra-Orthodox Jewish rabbi are not like the young people that you see hanging out in the food court at your local shopping mall. These young men were dressed very formally and wore ornate *yarmulkes,* had spirals of hair over their cheeks, twine hanging from their belts, and other visible symbols of their faith. I looked at the two and thought, "How unique." Then I looked down. Both were wearing Nike Air Jordan basketball shoes—loose and unlaced. "This is your culture," I thought. "You can run, but you cannot hide. Your culture is going to get you."

At that very moment another thought flashed into my mind. I remembered reading a newspaper article about a frightening trend in some inner-city neighborhoods where young people were being shot or mugged so that the mugger could steal their tennis shoes. The bottom line is that in some cases the value of a young human life is less than the cost of the shoes that they see on the feet of their television heroes.

Then I thought of another image. The Bible teaches that our feet are symbolic. How we walk says a lot about who we really are. And then I remembered the moment in C. S. Lewis's *The Chronicles of Narnia* in which the Christ-figure, Aslan, breathes on the feet of a giant who has been turned to stone in order to return him to life. "Don't worry," says the Great Lion, "once his feet have been set right, the rest will follow."

It is not a good sign, I decided, if the mass media that carry our popular culture have control of our feet, because that control may be symbolic of how we live.

Interpreting Media Signals

What I just did was take a media "signal"—a piece of secular information, a secular parable—and interpret it in biblical terms. My goal was to offer Christian images in response to an image from popular culture. I believe that our media are constantly sending out signals that can help the church go about its ministry and mission work in this post-Christian culture. Sadly, most of our churches and seminaries are ignoring both the content and social role of our mass media and the popular culture that they carry—which are among the most powerful forces in the modern world.

So what is a media signal? I have defined this as a single piece of media or popular culture focusing on a subject that is of interest to the church. It can be a newspaper article, a single episode of a television show, a compact disc, a movie, a new video, a best-selling book, or some other item.

The 1992 premiere of the television series "Star Trek: Deep Space 9" offers a perfect example of a theological signal from popular culture. In this episode, which was seen by about twenty million viewers, space station commander Benjamin Sisko tried to grasp the violence that was tearing apart the planet Bajor by seeking an audience with the high priestess, who served as the only source of Bajorian unity. In a temple filled with chanting monks in Buddhist-style robes, this holy woman framed the Federation officer's face with her hands and gazed into his eyes. "Have you ever explored your *pagh,* commander?" she said. "Bajorans draw courage from their spiritual life. Our life force, our *pagh,* is replenished by the prophets." The only hope for peace for himself and the planet was a spiritual breakthrough. Sisko, she said, had to find the Celestial Temple and the prophets who shaped Bajorian "theology." This was his destiny, his *pagh.* To help in his pilgrimage, the high priestess provided a glowing orb, shaped like the symbol for infinity, which had the supernatural ability to bend both time and space. Later, Sisko finally discovers the Celestial Temple and meets its godlike prophets, whose lives transcend linear time. Their ultimate message: "Look for solutions from within."

With its talk about life forces, theology, prophecy, a karma-like sense of destiny, and hints of reincarnation, "Deep Space 9" is philosophically murky, to say the least. The entire premiere episode is an assault on linear time. One secular critic said of this "Star Trek" series: "Go where no one has gone before and turn left."

Or perhaps we could say turn East. Consider that final message: "Look for solutions from within." This contrasts sharply with the Judeo-Christian emphasis on absolute truths, and a transcendent God. A Christian theologian from India, Vishal Mangalwadi, has told me that he sees many recurring Eastern themes in the "Star Trek" world. He calls this pop theology "Hollywood Hinduism."

This media signal is an example of a trend I believe the church cannot ignore. While I do not believe in conspiracy theories, I do believe that a kind of lowest-common-denominator religion exists in America's news and entertainment media and that it is much closer to the pantheism of Eastern religions than it is to the transcendent faith of orthodox Christianity.

Most seminary graduates—or at least those from seminaries who do not see apologetics as a form of intellectual bigotry—could do a much better job of debating a Buddhist on the nature of God than they could of debating the contents of an episode of "Star Trek" that focuses on the same theme. What good does it do us to know apologetics, to know systematic theology, to know our church's moral teachings, or to have mastered a host of other religious disciplines, if we cannot recognize when our culture beams theological and moral questions to us in the guise of entertainment? We cannot debate opponents if we do not listen to them, or take their viewpoints seriously.

Modern media constantly tell us stories and show us pictures. This frustrates church leaders. Stories offer lessons for life, but often in ways that are not logical or easy to translate. And besides, how can the church keep up with the waves of electronic media that flow through a typical American home in the space of a week, a month, a year? Thus, the church tends to ignore the social role and content of mass media. A typical pastor may stand in a pulpit and assume that his listeners understand sermons based on a Greek New Testament or a spiritual classic from the sixteenth century. But that same pastor will avoid dissecting the religious signals contained in a hit movie or television series because the entire congregation may not have seen it. This is one of many signs of a culture gap between the pulpit and the pews.

The point is this: for better and for worse, popular culture has spiritual and moral content. Popular culture offers the church a window into the subjects and images of daily life. Yes, the mirror of mass media is warped, at times. But this does not lessen the power of media to influence our culture. We must be critical as we tune into signals from the media. But all too often the church has little to offer in terms of informed insights into popular culture and the role that mass media play in daily life. I have found this to be just as true of churches on the left as on the right. It is true that many conservatives, and sometimes a few liberals, will attack the contents of specific shows. This is not enough. We cannot see popular culture's power because it is too obvious and too close to us. It is this closeness that blinds us. It is like the Chinese proverb, often quoted by media theorists, that says, "If you ask a fish to describe its life, it will not mention water." Water plays a role in their lives that is too big to see.

We swim in media. This is especially true of Americans born since World War II. Church growth researcher Lyle Schaller once told me that for young Americans media is not an influence on their culture—it is the only culture they share. In the future, everything young Americans know about their lives will have been shaped by the language, images, and styles they absorbed from media.

The Church and Popular Culture

Why does the church ignore the role that news and entertainment media play in our lives? I believe the church has tended to look at popular culture in five ways:

1. *Burn the culture.* This is the traditional approach of those on the religious right, the fundamentalists or separatists. Simply stated, it says, "When in doubt, burn it." This is especially true if there are television cameras nearby to record the scene. If the theological left ever uses this approach, it is almost always for reasons of elitism. Obviously, separatism is appropriate when dealing with many of the extreme forms of media that degrade women and children. But I do not believe this

should be the church's primary approach to popular culture. Today's media technologies are so pervasive and invasive that I believe we must understand how they work, and know something about their contents, even if we are going to create realistic strategies to help our people avoid them. I have been told that some members of Amish communities pay attention to trends in the modern world so that they can devise ways to avoid those very trends. You have to know something about automobiles to know you need to put red reflectors on the back of your buggies.

2. *Baptize the culture.* This approach is most often identified with the religious left. This view says that the culture is ahead of the church. The Bible is an out-of-date, culturally skewed book and its writers didn't understand life the way that we do today. Modern trends are the test of truth. Thus, the church attempts to change to fit the contents of the culture. Bishop William C. Frey of the Trinity Episcopal School for Ministry in Ambridge, Pennsylvania has called this "theology by opinion poll."

A case in point: If millions of teenagers want to have sex, then the Bible must be out-of-date in forbidding premarital sex. The left may also use this approach on issues of salvation or images of God, while the right often baptizes the culture on issues of economic and military issues.

When a church baptizes the culture it ends up with something that looks Christian with the culture soaked in. In many Episcopal and other mainline Protestant churches the liturgies look and sound the same, but the words have been redefined to mesh with the culture. The skin looks the same, but the heart has been changed.

3. *Photocopy the culture.* This is the dominant approach among modern evangelicals. The secular culture has radio, TV, and video. Thus, Christians have "Christian" radio, TV, and video. They have heavy metal and rap; Christians have heavy metal and rap. They have counseling and co-dependency books; ditto. They have aerobics classes; Christians have "firm believer" tapes. The secular world adores attractive superstars. So do Christians. Stop and think: how many megachurches

have short, fat, elderly, humorless senior pastors? The church rushes to offer its own version of each innovation by the popular culture.

This shadow culture serves many purposes, but it often leads to a retreat from any contact with the very culture the church is trying to reach. This is a strange approach to evangelism and mission. When modern megachurches use this approach the result is often the mirror image of that used in liberal churches. In this case, the rituals and words are changed, but the doctrinal core remains the same. The skin is changed, but the heart remains.

Note that this approach often fails to take seriously the ways in which media shape messages. A five-minute sermonette cannot deliver the content offered by a Charles Spurgeon sermon. In his *Amusing Ourselves to Death: Public Discourse in the Age of Show Business*, media critic Neil Postman has said that whatever Native Americans communicated by smoke signals, he doubts that they discussed abstract philosophy.[1] Jim and Tammy Bakker did not think that television would change them. It did.

4. Change the culture. Most of the time, we think of liberals or social gospel activists as the people who want to change culture through their own efforts. But please note that in the 1980s it was the theological right that stressed this approach. At times, conservatives seemed to think they could bring in the kingdom once they had signed up enough voters and locked up the right number of seats on the Supreme Court. I would be the last person to argue against Christians being involved in social causes. I would never suggest that the church should abandon what Reformed thinkers call the "cultural mandate" to work for change. All of God's creation is both good and fallen. We live with that tension. We cannot write off chunks of God's creation—such as politics, or the media—as beyond redemption. But, once again, what happens when this is the church's primary approach to culture? Often the result is a "save the world" posture.

5. Debate the culture. Simply stated, this is a missionary approach to culture. I believe that we live and work in a post-

Christian, missionary culture. Yet our churches rarely seem to be structured—emotionally or intellectually—to welcome evangelism and missions. All too often we are not interested in the practical issues of people's lives. Our blind spot on media and popular culture is evidence of a larger problem, a condition that I call "separation of church and life."

Don't hold your breath waiting for seminaries to help clergy wrestle with these issues. Here's the most cynical observation I can make about this situation: I am convinced our seminaries will require foreign missions majors to study the impact of American popular culture in the Third World before they require pastors to study the impact of media on the lives of people in American pews and neighborhoods.

Before we take a deeper look at a missionary approach to popular culture, I want to observe that many Christians use a sixth, and clearly nonbiblical, approach to mass media. This option is apathy. Many Christian leaders either ignore, or pretend to ignore, what is being said and done in mass media. They act as if they do not care about the role it plays in millions of lives. In my studies of the New Testament I have not found evidence anywhere of a biblical, Spirit-filled gift of apathy. The bottom line: I do not know why so many Christian leaders have decided that such powerful forces in modern life—the principalities and powers, if you will—do not need to be addressed by the church.

A Missionary Approach to Culture

A seminarian in my class was puzzled, if not alarmed. Why was it so important, he asked, for Denver Seminary students to learn how to analyze trends in the secular news and entertainment media? "Everyone knows," he said, "that the secular media are liberal and opposed to everything the church loves. So why take up classroom time trying to dissect signals from our popular culture?" After all, these were not the kinds of subjects that future pastors expected to study in their seminary years.

It was the spring of 1991 and I had been on the Denver Seminary campus for only two weeks as "Communicator on Culture." I knew I had some explaining to do. I told the class, "Pretend that I don't speak fluent evangelical. Tell me, in simple English, about a subject that really matters to seminary students."

A master of divinity student in the front row quickly answered: "Discipleship."

"Okay," I said. "What does 'discipleship' mean?"

He answered by saying that he wanted his ministry to touch people's real lives. He wanted to affect their views on the big issues of daily life—like marriage and money. "I want the faith to affect how they live," he said.

I agreed. Properly understood, discipleship will affect wallets, pocket calendars, couches, and bedrooms. Then I pointed at the blackboard, where I had written today's major forms of media, including television, advertising, movies, the news media, popular music and video, and various other print media. The secular media, I joked, have no influence on how Americans view jobs, success, sex, family, divorce, children, life, death, or eternity. People in our pews, and the unchurched, are never influenced by the media as they face these "big issues." And the folks who run the media never ignore or knock Christianity. Right? Looking around the classroom, I could see lights switching on.

It was while I was teaching and doing research on a seminary campus that I developed a three-part definition of discipleship for use in modern America. It consists of three questions: How do you spend your time? How do you spend your money? How do you make your decisions? If you can answer these questions without colliding with the power of the news and entertainment media, then you have a promising future in ministry to the Amish. They may be the only Americans whose lives will fit your approach to ministry and mission.

Yes, I admit that this is a secular, highly statistical definition of an important Christian term. But I believe that it offers insights into the lives of people in our pews and in the communities that our churches claim to want to reach. Consider, for a brief moment, the role that television plays in most American homes. At least one television set is turned on in the typical American home somewhere between thirty and fifty hours a week, depending upon the survey that is cited. Meanwhile, other studies have claimed that children may spend only a minute or less a day in communication with their fathers. Dr. Quentin Schultze of Calvin College has defined the American family as an economic unit made up of people who agree to live under the same roof for the purpose of paying their bills and watching television.

In *The Plug-In Drug*, Marie Winn makes another devastating observation. It is not children who are the primary television addicts, she says. Rather,

> it is their parents, fatigued by their offspring's incessant demands for learning in the broadest sense of the word (learning that may involve whining, screaming, throwing things, pestering), who require the "relaxation" afforded by setting the kids before the television screen and causing them to become, once again,...passive captives.[2]

Winn's thesis: Television is a drug administered by parents to their own children to make them docile, because, in the short run, that seems easier than raising the children themselves.

Is television a discipleship issue? Does it affect how people spend their time and money, and how they make their decisions? Is it an issue that the church should address? Stop and think about the typical den or family room. Any student of religious architecture would recognize the shapes of these rooms. Seating is arranged so that everyone can see through an empty vertical space that runs through the room. Everyone has a clear view of one crucial spot in the room, without having to turn their bodies in an uncomfortable manner. This is a religious sanctuary and, in the place of the Holy of Holies, sits the alternative altar known as the television.

If and when churches wake up and decide to address issues of media and popular culture, we must not allow these efforts to be focused only on children and young people. If we are honest, if we are missionaries who are concerned about people in this culture, then we must realize that these issues affect everyone, especially parents.

Consider one more specific issue: what is the number one complaint American wives have about their husbands? Watching football games on television is only a symptom of a larger communications issue. The boys who are trained to sit quietly and watch, watch, watch—in large part so that they won't destroy the house—tend to grow into passive men who think communication is a one-way activity that can be avoided by turning on a television. These men sit as trained, and their wives wonder why their husbands don't talk to them.

At this point seminary students almost always ask an important question. "Look, I'm confused," one will say. "Do you want us to watch more TV, or less TV?" My answer is simple: "I want you to watch less TV, but I want you to be awake while you're doing it."

Of course, there's more to it than that. As I said, I believe mass media carry signals that can offer church leaders insights into the strengths and weaknesses of secular faith proclaimed in popular culture. I believe we have to take media seriously enough to talk to people about the programs that influence them. We must ask young people about the superstars that influence their dress, speech, and beliefs. We must be prepared to talk to married couples about media issues in their relationships. We must learn about the lives of people who live in our mission field. Thus, I have developed a four-step process to help clergy and other church leaders think about specific media signals.

Step one is to select a specific media signal, as previously defined.

Step two is tricky and requires honest, open-minded analysis of this specific example of secular media. Our goal is to find the "secular subject" of that signal, as it might be defined by its secular creators. People who create popular culture must attract an audience. In one way or another they have to deal with real-life issues and they often do a better job at this task than church people do. Secular artists are forced to deal with the "big issues"—life, death, love, hate, money, marriage, sex, fear, children, anger, pride, hatred, war, and so forth. In step two, we need to ask: what was the subject that the artist wanted to address?

Step three is a mirror image of step two. Lo and behold, once you have found this secular subject, it will almost always have Christian and moral overtones. It will be a "sacred subject," a "big issue" that also drew the attention of saints and sinners in the Bible. At this point the church, marching through the centuries, can help us. Stories change. Images change. Questions often sound new and strange. But the "big issues" of life are remarkably constant, because the stuff of human experience is the same. Doctrines exist and the Bible speaks to each generation because the sacred subjects don't change. At this point, seminary-educated clergy and other church leaders are within shouting distance of daily life issues, as they are framed in popular culture.

Step four is the hardest part for most church leaders. At this point Christians need to think like missionaries and create ways in which the church can respond to specific signals. This does not require a television network or digital equipment. I believe the church must respond by using its strengths— preaching, Christian education, prayer groups, retreats, and other traditional forms of ministry.

But here is the key: it is crucial for church leaders to actually quote the signal as part of their response. We must talk to our people about the power the media play in their lives. We must quote Woody Allen on death. We must admit that we heard the voices of female anger in *Thelma and Louise*. We must tell parents the names of the other gods who are slipping into the world of Saturday morning television. When a cartoonist calls his work "Calvin and Hobbes," we need to laugh and explain to our people why this is theologically important.

Why is this so important? We must let women and men, girls and boys, know that the church cares about the forces that shape their lives. Like it or not, in modern America this means that the church must be prepared to debate the contents of the news and entertainment media. We cannot begin this debate, let alone conduct it in a critical manner, without studying signals from popular culture and then openly discussing them in the church. Church leaders who dare to do this will find that people want to discuss these subjects—a lot. They will not be dispassionate. They will challenge your opinions and criticize your judgments. They will pull you aside and bend your ear. They will ask questions. Many will ask for help. For many church leaders these reactions will be scary, at first. The church will have actually addressed a part of people's lives that matter to them. This is a reason to address media issues, not a reason to turn and run. We must fight the separation of church and life. Church leaders must admit that most of our people do not have the media under control. If anything, it is the other way around.

Listening to the Marketplace

> While Paul was waiting for them at Athens, he was deeply distressed to see that the city was full of idols. So he argued in the synagogue with the Jews and the devout persons, and also in the marketplace every day with those who happened to be there. (Acts 17:16-17)

The missionary was on the move during his first days in a city that defined truth for millions of people. He listened carefully in the public square, tuning in as old and new ideas collided. He talked with ordinary people, politicians, merchants, academics, and religious leaders about the choices that defined their lives. But mostly the missionary watched and listened as ordinary people went about their daily lives. He was interested in how they spent their time and their money. He cared about the ideas and forces that pulled at them as they made their decisions. It grieved him to see so many people surrendering their bodies, minds, and souls to idols. It seemed as if people were flirting with truth, competing to see who could try out the most new ideas and idols. Change was the true god. People rushed about and worshiped at many different idols and altars, some with names and some without. Finally, Athens' Powers That Be decided to hear what St. Paul had to say.

> Then Paul stood in front of the Areopagus and said, "Athenians, I see how extremely religious you are in every way. For as I went through the city and looked carefully at the objects of your worship, I found among them an altar with the inscription, 'To an unknown god.' What therefore you worship as unknown, this I proclaim to you." (Acts 17:22-23)

Paul was a missionary. Picture this. What would Paul see if he visited our shopping malls, offices, and schools? What if he spent time in our living rooms? What are the forces he would see shaping our popular culture and how we spend our time and money, and how we make our decisions?

In his remarks on Mars Hill, Paul argued that it is in God that "we live and move and have our being." In *All God's Children and Blue Suede Shoes*, media critic Kenneth Myers has noted that, for modern Americans, the truth would be more like: "In television, we live and move and have our being."[3] Today, many modern Americans vote for the presidential candidate who tells the best one-liners. Young people turn to rock stars, movies, and cable television for advice about private affairs and sexual decisions that, today, can be matters of life and death. Many parents allow their children to be raised by fictional characters. If real-life versions of many of these fleeting characters actually showed up on the doorstep, most parents would call 911.

This is our culture. Today's media are the merchants, politicos, and preachers who compete in the marketplace. Yet the church seems afraid to respond. Paul had courage and he didn't compromise. He spoke from a heart that ached because of what he had seen in markets, streets, temples, and homes. He did his homework and then preached with compassion and insight. He dared to recognize both the strengths and weaknesses of the culture around him. Paul listened to the voices in the marketplace. He paid attention to the images in the public square. Then, on Mars Hill, Paul was ready to debate for the hearts, minds, and souls of the lost.

What would Paul see and hear, if he visited our marketplace? How would he see us spending our time and money, and making our decisions? What would he say about how we are living our lives? Paul was a missionary and he founded missionary churches. Would Paul ignore the media?

Endnotes

1. Neil Postman, *Amusing Ourselves to Death: Public Discourse in the Age of Show Business* (New York: Penguin, 1985), p. 7.

2. Marie Winn, *The Plug-In Drug* (New York: Penguin, 1985), p. 55.

3. Kenneth Myers, *All God's Children and Blue Suede Shoes* (Wheaton, Ill.: Crossway Books, 1989), p. 160.

Nan Peete

New Wine for New Wineskins

IN THE AUGUST 9 issue of *Newsweek,* the statement was made that one thousand "dissatisfied" Episcopalians were descending upon St. Louis. However, like Jane Dixon, I am not one of the thousand dissidents. I have not met any here so far. If there are dissidents here, then they have been mighty quiet. Of course, I cannot imagine anyone paying his or her own way to come to St. Louis just to gripe. If you are like me, you love and care for the church. That is why you are here and that is why I am here.

In order to give you a frame of reference for my remarks, I want to tell you a little bit about myself. I am a fourth-generation Episcopalian. My dad was confirmed in 1911 using the 1892 Prayer Book. My children and grandchildren are baptized Episcopalians. I grew up in the diocese of Chicago and my experience of the Episcopal Church there was of a black church. St. Thomas', my home parish, is over one hundred years old, and is the mother church to black Episcopalians. At the time I was growing up, St. Edmund's, a neighboring church, had a large elementary school as well as an active parish. Trinity Episcopal Church was the other neighboring parish. All three were black congregations. While aware of the larger church, we had little or no contact with white congregations except for visits from the bishop and some white clergy who assisted periodically. St. Thomas' was an Anglo-Catholic parish, with Saturday confessions and Solemn High Mass on Sunday morning. I moved to Los Angeles in 1970, and have since lived in five of our dioceses and have attended the General Seminary in New

York, so my experience of the Episcopal Church has broadened since those days in Chicago.

I have found the subtitle of our conference of interest: "A Grassroots Forum on Episcopal Structures." As one who has done community organizing, I understand "grassroots" to refer to people who are without power, but among those attending this conference are many who have been in decision-making positions. I have seen bishops, bishops-to-be, deans, seminary professors, clergy, deputies to General Convention, members of vestries, leaders and members of diocesan or national church committees, and diocesan staff folk. If we are the grassroots, then who are the branches and the leaves? There seems to be a lot of power here to me.

From my perspective, I think we are asking the wrong question, or asking the question prematurely. The question should not be, "What should the structures be?" but rather, "What is the mission of the church in the future?" Structure should follow mission, not the other way around. Form follows function. I think the real issue is that we are unclear as to what our mission truly is.

The outline of faith in our Book of Common Prayer says, "The mission of the church is to restore all people to unity with God and each other in Christ." It further states, "The church pursues its mission as it prays and worships, proclaims the Gospel, and promotes justice, peace, and love." The church then carries this mission out "through the ministry of all its members." We are all familiar with that mission statement. We put it in our materials and on our letterheads, but I am not sure that we agree on how to do it. For years Episcopalians have been known as the "frozen chosen." However, I prefer thinking of us as the "thawed and flawed." We have also said, "If you want to be an Episcopalian, you already are one." Our churches are sometimes nestled in secluded neighborhoods behind lush shrubbery with discreet signs where only the elect are able to find them. They are places of good order and good taste, literate, rational, and reserved. Is this our mission? I would like to share a few reflections about what I think our mission is and what the implications and ramifications of that mission might be for some of our structures, institutions, and traditions.

In the brochure announcing this conference, the inside of the front page stated, "It's time to face the issues. They are as plain as black and white." Underneath is the chart showing the decrease in the numbers of Episcopalians over the last twenty-five years while the population in the United States has increased. After looking at those figures in the brochure, I called the U.S. Census Department to get a breakdown of the population over the past three decades, and I received a document from them that shows the changes in population by race and ethnic origin. In the decade of the sixties, the white population increased 11.9 percent; it increased 6 percent in the seventies and in the eighties. The black population in the sixties increased 19.7 percent, in the seventies 17.3 percent, and in the eighties 13.2 percent. The American Indian, Eskimo, and Aleut population in the decade of the sixties increased 50 percent, in the seventies 71.7 percent, and in the eighties 37.9 percent. The Asian and Pacific Islander population in the decade of the sixties increased 75.3 percent, in the seventies 127.5 percent, and in the eighties 107.8 percent. For persons of Hispanic origin, the figures from the sixties are not available because of a redefinition, but in the seventies that population increased 61 percent, and in the eighties 53 percent.

The Census Bureau's information also showed the percentage of the total population each one of these racial and ethnic groups represented. In 1970 the white population represented 83.5 percent of the total; by 1990, it had declined to 75.6 percent. The black population rose from 11.1 percent of the total population in 1970 to 12.1 percent in 1990. The American Indian, Eskimo, and Aleut population also rose slightly, from 0.4 percent in 1970 in 1980 to 0.8 percent in 1990, while the Asian and Pacific Islander population showed a marked increase, from 0.7 percent in 1970 to 2.9 percent in 1990. Likewise, persons of Hispanic origin increased from 4.5 percent of the population in 1970 to 9 percent in 1990.

Clearly, our population mix is changing. Doing and understanding mission and ministry in this new and rapidly changing and pluralistic society is not easy. Sometimes it makes us want to stay in the boat that Loren Mead talked about. How has the Episcopal Church responded to these changes? Prior to 1973, there were 13 Episcopal congregations and missions to Asian Americans in five dioceses: California, Hawaii, Los Angeles, Maryland, and Olympia. Since 1973, 41 new Asian-American congregations have been established in 16 additional dioceses, and there are now 39 Asian-American clergy. In 1991, there were 91 congregations in the contiguous eight provinces with Hispanic ministries. There were approximately 400 African-American congregations and approximately 500 African-American clergy, including those who are retired.

I must say that it has been surprising for me to come here and see so few persons of color represented at this conference. I wonder why. I have three reasons I would like to suggest. First, many were unable to take time off from their jobs and could not afford the cost. Even though many persons of color are middle class, we are also salaried employees who do not have control over all of our time except for vacation. Second, people involved in this conference from the 96 dioceses represented did not make an effort to encourage or support minority participation. Third, many persons of color are not particularly interested in the issue of church structures since they have not been a part of the institutional system; they are more interested in doing mission and want to spend their time and priorities there. For many, including me, talk of change in structures and decentralization arising from the East Tennessee Initiative conjures up images that we last heard when people were talking about structure and states' rights.

Before I went to seminary I worked for three years as a management consultant for Coopers and Lybrand in Los Angeles. As one of the managers in the department would tell us when we went on a new assignment, "Do not see this as a problem to be solved. Look on it as an opportunity to succeed." I see the drop in the number of Episcopalians and the increasingly pluralistic population as an opportunity for mission, an opportunity to expand the circle, to welcome all to the table. We can learn and be enriched by others. They have something to offer.

If we do not open our hands and hearts to welcome, we cannot receive. A closed hand is turned in on itself. If we do not offer that hand, we will be irrelevant. Changing structures without changing mission will be like rearranging the deck chairs on the Titanic.

We have the gifts and the tools to implement this mission. It is found in our baptismal covenant that we renew and are renewed by throughout our liturgical year. I would like to share my understanding of what that covenant means.

In the baptismal covenant we say that, with God's help, we will "continue in the apostles' teaching and fellowship, in the breaking of bread, and in the prayers." We Episcopalians continue in the teaching and fellowship well, with spirit and with passion. However, we can sometimes focus all of that energy on ourselves. We are so glad to see one another that we forget the visitor. As much as we like to use the family metaphor, sometimes our family is a closed system. When we translate our home to our church we sometimes only invite to the Lord's table those we invite to our dining table. We are the community of faith, a people of prayer, and it is from communion that we are a community.

We then say we will "persevere in resisting evil," and when we sin we will "repent and return to the Lord." This can only happen if we are a people of prayer and break bread together. We all fall short—individually, collectively, institutionally. I guess those Saturday confessions as a teenager have left a lasting impression on me, since confession is still a necessary part of my spiritual and prayer discipline. We also need to repent as an institution. We need to repent of our sins of racism, sexism, and classism. We need to return to the Lord. In God's abundant graciousness to us, we have unlimited opportunities to repent of our sins against one another and against God.

The promises in the covenant get harder as we go along. The third promise says that with God's help we will "proclaim by word and example the Good News of God in Christ." We promise to be evangelists. How do we by our word and example proclaim the good news? Do we really invite our friends and families to church? Do we share what is going on in our parishes with others, and if not, why not? What would happen if three million Episcopalians did "bumper sticker" evangelism with that sign that says, "The Episcopal Church Welcomes You"? With most of us having more than one car, that sticker could be on six million cars! What a statement that would make, especially at the malls around Christmas time. Do we live our lives during the week in such a way that others around us will know that we are Christians, much less Episcopalians?

The next promise: with God's help we will "seek and serve Christ in all persons," and we will love our neighbors as ourselves. Part of the problem is that we don't love ourselves. We must seek and serve in all persons. Each of us is a miniature global village. Our cars come from Europe and Japan, our clothes from Paris or Hong Kong or the sweatshops of Central America, our fruit and coffee from South America. We are our neighbor. What happens overseas or across the river affects what happens to us. What happened in Florida last year, or South Carolina the year before, or the midwest where we are today affects us all. A newscast during one of the most critical times in the floods came from the town of Alton, Illinois. The bridge had not held, and the town was isolated. The mayor was telling the reporter, "We survived. Our structure is in place and things seem to be okay." But while he was talking, in the background you could see trucks filling up with water for the people in Des Moines. The people in Alton were helping others who also needed help. Our neighbor is everyone. Some have said that Episcopalians "seek and serve" better than any other denomination. We run more shelters, soup kitchens, food pantries, and AIDS ministries than all other denominations combined. We can brag a little or maybe even a lot sometimes. Yet we see more and more need.

There is a story of a group of campers fishing by the stream. They saw a body floating by, so one of them stopped and rushed in to rescue it. That body was no sooner retrieved than another came floating by. Pretty soon there were so many bodies that everyone had to quit fishing and spend all their time rescuing bodies from the stream. Eventually some of them stopped their rescuing and started to walk up to the head of the stream. They realized that they needed to stop those who were throwing the bodies in. That is a move from charity to justice, which brings us to the last promise in the baptismal covenant.

We say we will "strive for justice and peace among all people, and respect the dignity of every human being." I think that those who assembled the baptismal covenant, in their infinite wisdom, knew the relationship of a life of prayer to community. We continually repent and return to the Lord in order to proclaim by word and example the good news; only in this way can we love our neighbor and finally strive for justice and peace, and respect the dignity of every human person. We know there is no peace without justice and no justice without the respect for every human person. There are no qualifiers of person, whether of race, color, sexual orientation, ethnic origin, ordained or lay. All are made in the image of God.

These five promises of our baptismal covenant are our marching orders for mission in this increasingly pluralistic society. As we look at this mission we may and do need to look at some of our structures, institutions, and traditions and see how they impede or hinder our mission. The list is more extensive than I can examine at present. However, I will focus on several.

We need to look at our seminaries. How is the mission of the church in the future being enhanced and enabled by the curriculum, the cost, the faculty at our seminaries? Our seminaries do a great job. I graduated from one. I received an honorary degree from another, and I am on the board of the one from which I graduated. I also coordinate our ordination process in the diocese of Atlanta. I am very aware and involved in our seminary education process. Still I ask, are we preparing clergy to minister in this new world? Are we looking at alternative paths to the classical seminary education—alternatives that do not mean they are second class? Are we including cross-cultural studies? Or are we just preparing our clergy to care for those of us who are already in the boat?

What about our structures for meetings? In the diocese of Atlanta, most if not all of our diocesan meetings take place between 10 and 2 o'clock on Tuesday, Wednesday, or Thursday. That limits those who can participate. When I was in the diocese of Indianapolis, most of our meetings took place on Saturday and in the evenings, including those sacred meetings like Standing Committee and Commission on Ministry and even Finance. That allowed participation to include more than those with time on their hands or who lived or worked near the diocesan offices. I am sure there are more dioceses like Atlanta than Indianapolis.

At the 1988 Lambeth Conference, Bishop Okulu of Kenya talked about his need to do mission differently depending on the community in which he was going to be involved. He said he could not do the same thing in every tribal community or in every urban community because different communities required different skills and different ways of getting the message across. We must not be afraid to try new ways to minister with one another. At that Lambeth Conference one of the largest contingents of bishops was from the continent of Africa. I am sure that at the next one they will be in the majority. The increasing number of Anglican Christians on the continent of Africa is a direct result of the increasing indigenization of its clergy and its leadership.

Deployment of clergy is still a difficult issue for us. Who gets placed where? We all know what most of us want in our congregations. We want someone to lead us who looks like us, thinks like us, talks like us, and believes like us. We need to look at who we are calling for mission to help us in our mission and in our ministry.

We need to examine life tenure for clergy. I know I've "gone to meddling" with that one. We have (and as I say, I have been in five dioceses) wonderful congregations that are alive and dynamic with clergy who have been there for many years. But we have some congregations—more than we would like to admit—that are languishing and whose people are hungry. How do we address those issues? We need to look at that.

We need to look at how we do continuing education for the new mission of the church. The church today is not the same as the church in which I was confirmed in 1948, yet not all clergy have continued their education and developed their spiritual life to meet the opportunities presented by change. We need to seek and provide programs of continuing education to facilitate this. I know the Cornerstone Project is doing just that.

The last item on the list that I would like to note is our need to take a serious look at the vocation to the episcopate. We know priests who want to be bishops. Why not prepare them in advance? On-the-job training is costly. Priests also develop some inappropriate ways to seek the office and later carry those ways into the office once they are elected. At the examination in the service of ordination, these new bishops respond to the questions placed to them as if they had been prepared for that ministry long before the election, yet there is no vehicle for preparing them for the episcopate.

The issues confronting bishops and their ministry demand attention, and there are other structures, institutions, and traditions that need another look. Of course, we should always be looking at our institutions and structures. We should be living in a dynamic way instead of a static mode. The structures are there to serve the mission. Once we are clear about the mission, the structures will be easier to define.

What, you may be asking, does this have to do with the title of my presentation, "New Wine for New Wineskins"? The opportunities for mission are the new wineskins of our various colors, hues, shapes, and sizes. To pour old wine into them— even highly prized vintages such as Solemn Evensong from the 1662 Prayer Book as at the cathedral in Atlanta—does not taste good to everyone. Even to some of us in old skins. The taste can be developed, but new wine is also good. To put new wine into old, cracked wineskins may cause the wineskins to break or cause the particles to contaminate the new wine.

According to a story, there was a young man who was the most disreputable character in town and who ran with the wrong crowd. One day he saw an attractive woman and he tried to court her. She rebuffed him, so he decided to trick her. He went and found a mask. It was the mask of a saint. He pretended to be the saint in order to win the woman's hand. And so he did: he succeeded in marrying her. Sometime later he ran into some of his former friends who knew what he had done. They said, "We are going to expose you as a fake and make you take off your mask in front of your wife." Sure enough, the next time he and his wife were together and his friends saw him, they approached him and forced him to remove his mask. As the mask fell to the ground his friends were shocked, for they saw the face of a saint. He had become what he had pretended to be.

In this diet-conscious society, we are all well aware that "we are what we eat." Week by week, day by day we eat the body and drink the blood of our savior Jesus Christ. Week by week, day by day we become more what we eat. It is only when the bread is broken that it can feed. It is only when the wine is poured out that it can nourish. It is only when we are broken into the world, when we walk out of the boat or the nave that we can feed and nourish those in the world. We have been given through the renewal of our baptism vows a new anointing as Christ's light in the world. We have been given a new attitude for mission, a new awareness of who we are and Whose we are, and a new agenda for carrying out that mission. For *we* are the new wine and the new wineskins.

Nelle Bellamy

The Church and Changing Times

THIS TOPIC CALLS UP a host of voices and images in the Episcopal Church at the close of the twentieth century. One might wish that amid the rapidly changing national scene and the problems of the nations of the world the church would be a less chaotic place, one in which we might say our prayers, worship God, and serve in the world. For some of us these are exciting times; for others the response is confusion, despair, and even anger, because change brings conflict.

What a wide range of images and voices we see and hear! We hear the joy of newly ordained women priests and bishops. We hear the angry voices of parishes that do not want women clergy on their staffs. We feel the anguish of women clergy as they meet opposition in many parts of the church. With the image of the national church structure a great crowd of voices and emotions are evoked. I recently read an account of a visit to the Church Center by a communicant of St. David's parish in Austin, Texas. She wrote, "Everyone in this building is working hard to make sure that the prayers and wishes of St. David's family and other Episcopal Church families are carried out....If there is any doubt in your mind about our National Church offices, rest assured that the people I encountered were kind, dedicated people who want to serve God's people."

I can recall my experiences as an archivist at the Church Center. In inventorying the records created in the offices there I learned what the staff did and how they went about it. I encountered many hard-working, dedicated people who viewed their jobs as vocations in the church. Alongside these positive images we see the negative ones. We hear the criticisms of the House of Bishops and the Presiding Bishop. We can feel the pain at the national church offices as many dioceses refuse to support programs of the church by withholding their quotas. Strong voices and emotions emerge as the church tries to understand the issue of the ordination of active homosexuals. There are voices for and against. We can feel the hurt and anger. I have chosen only a few voices and images in our church today. There are many others.

The question before us and before the whole church, however, is, "How do we serve God in his church as we are surrounded by change?" Is it enough to snuggle down in our parishes, say our prayers, and be concerned about the social issues in our local neighborhoods? I think not! We do not have this option!

Obviously the situation demands our attention and our concern. I do not think for one moment, however, that despair should be our response. Nor should we allow our perspectives to be distorted. The church is larger than my parish of St. John's in Johnson City, Tennessee. It is larger than the diocese of East Tennessee. It is larger than the Episcopal Church, larger even than the world-wide Anglican Communion of which we are a part. And yet it is difficult to live in these times when older patterns seem to be fading, when theological positions with which we may disagree abound, and when some of us may be unable to worship with a new prayer book.

The early church was a rough place in which to be a Christian. The fourth and fifth centuries in which the theological positions on the Incarnation and the Trinity were hammered out in the councils of the church were, it seems to me, far more troublesome than our present times. For example, there was theological warfare among the bishops of the sees in the East. In Alexandria, there were strong bishops with finely-honed political skills that were not always ethically appropriate. When one of the bishops of Alexandria needed support for a theological issue he would send word to the monks in the deserts along the Nile River that the doctrine of the exalted role of the Mother of our Lord was being questioned. Since this doctrine was very important for them, the desert monks would flock in to support the bishop on his current theological stance. As far as I can discern, no bishop in this church has tried such political tactics. One can imagine, however, what might have happened if certain bishops had had pious desert monks outside their see cities.

As we examine the Episcopal Church, it is obvious that we are today fraught with joy and sadness, love and anger, and the whole range of emotional responses. As I considered this I looked back over the years since June 1959, when I began working with the archives of the General Convention and the Executive Council. I was on the payroll of the General Convention from June 1959 until my retirement in July 1992. I have been a part of the national structure. Thank God, however, I lived in Texas rather than New York City. The years were painful and joyful. It was never easy to defend an archives budget to the Joint Standing Committee on Program, Budget, and Finance. I was happy to be a part of the national church staff; I considered the position of archivist as a vocation in God's church. I tried not to become too much of a bureaucrat. I believe that in some way, which I certainly do not understand, God's grace is present in the church's politics and in her institutional affairs. I say all of this to give you some insights into who I am as I look at our church-in-change in my remaining remarks.

Are you able to look with me at some of the outstanding changes in the Episcopal Church in the past thirty years and not, for the moment, take sides on the issues? May I describe these issues as if I were someone on the sidelines or someone from another planet? Personally I have strong positions on these issues and I feel certain that you do, too. Can we, nevertheless, be descriptive for a moment?

The General Convention Special Program is a good place to begin. Historians of the church through the years will examine this program and its impact. It pretty much turned the church upside down. We are told that Bishop Hines walked the streets of Harlem in New York City and from this experience came his powerful influence on the church. Like an Amos or Jeremiah with his stirring southern oratory, he called on the Episcopal Church to recognize the great numbers of black people who had few empowerment skills and who did not feel at home in the culture or in our church. Large portions of the operating funds of the national church were allocated to this program at the General Convention of 1969. The women of the church designated UTO grant money for the Triennial to the General Convention Special Program. What was the result of this effort among the communicants throughout the church? There were strong supportive responses and there were those who, though not necessarily against the program, did not approve of the way it was administered. Finally many of the dioceses refused to pay their quotas and fifty percent of the Church Center staff lost their jobs.

Then came the struggle for the ordination of women. The House of Bishops passed the legislation with only a few dissenting members, but the House of Deputies had more difficulties and barely passed the required canonical change. However, there has been steady movement on this issue, despite its heated beginnings. According to recent statistics from the Anglican Consultative Council, there were 788 women deacons, 1031 women priests, and one woman bishop in 1992. There are now three women bishops. And yet many of our ordained women continue to be faced with open and more veiled opposition. Because of the traditional catholic doctrine of a male priesthood, our ordained women have faced difficulties not present within our more Protestant sister churches. Debates about human sexuality followed, fueled particularly by the discussions surrounding the ordination of active homosexuals. We are today bombarded on all sides by the arguments for and against. And not only have we encountered powerful social issues and witnessed changes in our midst, in 1979 the General Convention gave final approval to a new prayer book. Acceptance has not been unanimous.

Look at all of this. Within a thirty-year period the Episcopal Church has changed in important areas of its life. Some of us have joyfully hailed what is believed to be an awakening of the church in the second half of the twentieth century. Others have been saddened and pained as the church which they knew and loved seems to have set itself on different paths.

Various responses have emerged in the church as we have tried to live with these changes and in a number of cases there have been strong negative reactions. A number of groups have broken away from the church, calling themselves "continuing churches." Other actions have been taken in response to other changes. The Prayer Book Society continues its efforts to preserve the 1928 Book of Common Prayer. There is also the dissatisfaction with the national church offices and the movement to withhold funds from them. The General Convention meeting in Phoenix, Arizona in 1988, faced with falling revenues, mandated that the staff at the Church Center be cut and that the budget for salaries be reduced by $1 million. These cuts have taken place and it was a very painful process. Later, as the quotas continued to fall behind, other adjustments were made. This time they were in the program budget. Apparently the money problems have not been solved and there is great unrest as the Church Center staff fears additional rounds of reductions.

What can we say about all of this? We can certainly emphasize that the Episcopal Church is not alone in the Anglican Communion as it faces new challenges. The issue of the ordination of women is evoking strong reactions in the Church of England. The church is now faced with the consideration of how those who cannot accept the ordination of women can live in the Church of England. The discussion about nongeographical dioceses has made recent headway. There are clergy and parishes who declare that they cannot worship with a woman priest presiding at the Eucharist. We read that at least two hundred fifty Anglican clergy will seek a home in the Roman Catholic Church. Other parts of the Anglican Communion are faced with disturbing issues. For example, our fellow Anglicans in the provinces of Central and South America are asking about the relevance of an English tradition to their Latin cultures. African churches have different pressing problems than we in the United States. They must deal with the spread of Islam. This was very obvious at the most recent Lambeth Conference when the African bishops spoke.

I do not think that the drastic measures of withdrawal from the Episcopal Church or from Anglicanism are a viable option. Neither do I think that withholding funds from an already anxious staff at the Church Center is appropriate. I also think that there are good reasons for some kind of central organization at the national level that can act for all of us in ecumenical matters, in missionary outreach, as well as in certain overall responsibilities within the church. As the Anglican Communion seems to be coming of age when our planet seems to grow smaller and smaller, the Episcopal Church needs a national organization for relationships with Anglican churches in other nations.

What can I say to those who are active, dedicated communicants in this church of ours and are seeking for some kind of positive word in these changing times? We know that the nation and the world are in a period of upheaval—how well we know this! We long to turn to the church for solace and a bit of peace; we long to worship and not be disturbed by all that surrounds us. We may, even, long to be insulated in our parish life from all the troublesome voices of the times. We realize that such isolationism is not possible if we fulfill our Christian responsibilities. As Christians we are the body of Christ *and* also citizens in the nation and the world.

The Roman Catholic Church in Vatican II emphasized the biblical concept of the church as a pilgrim in this world moving toward a heavenly home. Is this imagery at all useful? It does *not* require that we sell all of our property and dismantle our institutional structures. Can we not think of ourselves as a pilgrim band in this modern world—a pilgrim band with an institutional structure, but also with the hope and trust that God is at work in his church if we only stop to realize this? God has not left us alone. We are nourished by the sacraments; we are accompanied by fellow pilgrims in the Way. Can we not seek to become informed, to try to avoid too much anger and not to be overly swayed by our emotions? Given the fact that we are all baptized sinners, this may be impossible. It is, however, what we are called to be.

An example of the church and changing times is seen in the life of a laywoman who lived in the fourteenth and early fifteenth centuries in England. She is Julian of Norwich, or simply, Mother Julian. She lived a solitary life in a little cell attached to her parish church, where pilgrims visited her. When I went to this place hallowed by devotion and great dedication a few years ago, I found a little card there that reads: "I saw that [God] is at work unceasingly in every conceivable thing, and that it is all done so well, so wisely, and so powerfully that it is far greater than anything we can imagine, guess, or think." You have, no doubt, encountered the thought of Mother Julian, as many have referred to her feminine language for members of the Trinity. Have you also heard these well-known words?

> All will be well, and all will be well, and every kind of thing will be well....[It] seemed to me impossible that every kind of thing should be well....And to this I had no other answer as a revelation from our Lord except this: what is impossible to you is not impossible to me.[1]

Why these references to Mother Julian's theology? They speak, it seems to me, to twentieth-century men and women who live with change. The God whom she knew loved all of his creatures—all of his children. Mother Julian's world, however, was full of pain and suffering, while the church seemed to emphasize hell and doom more than love and joy. Mother Julian could not resolve this paradox. She lived with it, trusting that in some way, in some time, God will make all things well. A. M. Allchin, a canon of the Church of England, has referred to Mother Julian as a voice for today as we live in times which we do not understand. We, like Mother Julian, must trust God and believe that in some fundamental ways God is in the church and the world.

Mother Julian's response was to live in the paradox of that which she did not understand and the great love of God for his children. We today, whether or not we articulate it, can and do live with change. To say that "all will be well" is not a simplistic, sentimental, Pollyanna approach to life. No! It is a response of great trust in God's love for his people as they live in the world and the church. Mother Julian's experience of God was one of hope as she looked at her world. She believed that in some way, at some time, God would make all well. *When*, she does not know! *How*, she does not know! Trusting in the loving God of her great experiences, she could live with uncertainty as she realized that what is impossible to us is not impossible to God.

As I close these remarks, it is obvious that I have been talking about attitudes. I have no great plan to superimpose on this church. My concern is how we, with all of our diversity, exist in God's church. Change will continue; the church is not static. How do we live out our Christian commitment? The image of a pilgrim church and the great faith and trust of Mother Julian have been useful for me and helped me to maintain a perspective centered in God's great love for his children. I recommend them, therefore, to you.

Endnotes

1. From chapters 27 and 233 of the long text of Julian of Norwich in *Showings,* trans. Edmund Colledge and James Walsh (New York: Paulist Press, 1978).

Part Four

The Challenge of Leadership

D iscussion of the nature of leadership is a natural part of a symposium organized around the topic of church structure: for many, the most visible part of the church is its leaders. However, those speakers who examined the question of leadership in the light of the church's changing context focused less on critique of the present and more on the needed adaptations for the future.

In our section on ministry we have already presented some of those thoughts, particularly with attention to the ministry of bishops. The papers in this section represent a different approach. The first two bring learnings from the contemporary world of business to the situation of the church. If the corporate world outside is changing, what might it have to say to the church? Is there a relationship between the revolutions taking place in the corporate world and the teachings of the gospel? The last piece turns back to the church, with a focus on the gospel mission. It is a vision of leadership at its very heart.

Steven Rottgers is vicar of Christ the King Episcopal Church in Poquoson, Virginia. He has previously served as an associate rector on the staffs of two large churches and as the founding chairman of the diocesan Congregational Development Commission in Southern Virginia. He has recently joined in a cooperative effort to form the Quality Mutual Ministry

Institute, a ministry dedicated to fostering a greater understanding and use of Edward Deming's theories of quality and
management in the life of the church. His presentation provides an introduction and overview of Deming's theories and
suggestions for how they might be applied in the local parish.

George Lockwood has been active as a layman at all levels
of the Episcopal Church over the past twenty-five years. He
has served on vestries and bishops' committees; as senior war-
den; on diocesan councils in several dioceses, including as
president; as chairman of Venture in Mission; on standing
committees; on bishop search committees, including vice-
chairman of the nominating committee for the Presiding
Bishop; as trustee and chairman of a seminary; as a deputy to
General Convention since 1976; and on the Executive Council
and its committee for long-range planning. His paper focuses
on the changes needed for leadership toward "God's preferred
future." He explores creative ways for the people of God to fulfill their call to be "ecclesiastical entrepreneurs."

Tony Campbell is Canon Missioner of the diocese of South
Carolina. He has served previously as vicar of Holy Cross-Faith
Memorial and St. Cyprian's in Georgetown, South Carolina as
well as rector of Baskerville Ministries on Pawley's Island. A
gifted preacher and teacher, he presents a moving case for a renewed leadership in the church of the future. His piece, rooted
in the gospel message, serves as a fitting conclusion to this
presentation of the work done in St. Louis. His hope and
prayer is that St. Louis will be the beginning point of action,
and he closes with a call for courage in following Christ.

Steven R. Rottgers

Rethinking Parish Structures: The Quality Questions

IT WAS THE SUMMER of my twelfth year as an ordained priest and I was frustrated. The questions which abounded in my head begged for answers that worked.

—Why do chronic problems continue to haunt and frustrate churches?

—Why is it hard to motivate and direct staff members or lay participants in churches?

—Why do "best efforts" always seem to fall short of set goals and cause more problems in other areas?

—Why do budgets and numerical goals seem to dominate vestry priorities and remain unmanageable?

—Why do a few good people carry the burden of the majority of church members most of the time?

—Why do churches experience in-fighting, a boardroom mentality on the vestry, a fear of authority, and an "I can't do that" attitude?

I realized that my frustrations were similar to those of many church leaders who had gone before me. It could be that similar frustrations are part of the reason you are here today in St. Louis. Maybe you have similar, painful questions.

At around this time last year, my wife gave me a book about Dr. W. Edward Deming that initiated a journey for me. Deming's name has been prominently associated with the revolution in quality throughout the world, beginning in Japan, where his theories were first applied, and later, by force of suc-

cess, in his own country, the United States. Today he is recognized as perhaps the foremost management expert in developing systems for quality and success. I was interested in the
answers he might offer for the church. What I read of his management theories made sense, and I spent time applying them
to the church understood as a service organization. It was the
beginning of a journey of enlightenment. Deming's principles
made sense of frustrating behaviors and repeated patterns of
failure. His solutions also made sense. I believe that, with some
adaptation, Deming's work holds both insight and direction
for changes which are badly needed in the management of the
modern parish church.

It has been all too easy for the church to dismiss the insights
of business management as too "secular." However, we need to
remember that the barriers separating sacred and secular are
often artificial. God calls us to be "whole," balanced in mind,
body, and spirit. All three are needed and are present at all
times and in all places, whether in the church or the secular
world. The whole of our experience can and should be brought
to bear within the life of the church. In the same manner, our
spiritual lives should enter and influence our workplaces and
our homes. To fulfill the potential to which God has called us
requires the whole of who we are. The sharing of the good
news should be a two-way street: just as we carry the good
news of Christ into the world, so too, we should carry the
good news of the world into the church.

Deming's famous Fourteen Principles of Effective Management can be seen as nothing less than a structure for facilitating a biblical work ethic in the modern workplace. It is
interesting and worth noting that Deming, a member of St.
Paul's, Washington, D.C. and one of the most influential Episcopal laymen outside the church, has largely been ignored
within the managerial life of the church. It can be argued that
we shouldn't try to bring work issues into the church, and
managerial theory can be seen as deficient in theological commitment or insight. However, we need to remember that issues
of organizational structures are an essential part of Scripture.
Jethro's advice to his son-in-law, Moses, on how to organize

the leadership of Israel is perhaps the earliest example of a manager creating a system to meet the needs of a group of people (Exod. 18:13-27). In the book of Acts, we have yet another example of a new system—a new church and its leadership—responding to the voice of its "customers," the people of God, creating innovations which met their legitimate needs. The Hellenistic widows were being neglected and a need had arisen within the church. The answer was to delegate a team of seven new ministries, the "deacons," to explore the need and to respond. The perceived *fracturing* of leadership instead facilitated the *empowerment* of a broader ministry base, thereby fostering both spiritual and numerical growth (Acts 6:1-7).

Jesus himself offers a basis for understanding managerial relationships throughout his teachings. He repeatedly engaged in very focused leadership training for his disciples, particularly Peter, James, and John. Jesus practiced the "Pareto Principle" centuries before it was recognized by modern business.[1] He was confident in his ministry to a small, selected group of leaders, and was not dominated by anxieties about the many who could not be ministered to by a single individual. He was willing to concentrate his efforts on the small percentage who would become leaders, investing his energy in the later outcome of his actions. Jesus saw situations "holistically" rather than in a fragmented, analytical fashion. His larger perspective revealed the difference between "gnats" and "camels."

St. Paul argues in favor of what Deming would describe as "systems thinking" in his understanding of the need for cooperative effort in successful situations. Paul's analogy of the church as a body consisting of many parts, united in the one Spirit, possessing unique gifts, separate yet dependent upon harmony and the existence of others for health, is a profound summary of the nature of all healthy systems (1 Cor. 12:4-28).

Today, the primary reason for the rejection of mixing business practices with church practices is the past track record of that mixture. The frustration, disappointment, pain, disillusionment, and repeated failures often associated with the practice of business within the church is a judgment on a flawed *method* of conducting business which industry itself is now rejecting. It should not be seen, however, as a failure of business within the church. The church can no more avoid the use of business practices than it can cease to be in the world. The question is whether our business and managerial practices will reflect the gospel and further its aims, or continue to be a hindrance to the success of the modern church.

The methods which have dominated the business and management practices of the church over the better part of this century are an adaptation of the "assembly line" mentality articulated by Frederick Taylor in his theory of "Scientific Management" at the turn of the century.[2] This model was very much the standard for all of the mainline denominations. It is a managerial understanding designed to produce Model T's. The results of this model, however, have been the robbing of the workers' creativity, pride, and enthusiasm. This "Management By Objectives" was created by management to keep workers working and productive. Managers managed, workers worked, and the two never mixed. This system was imported into the church from the larger culture of the business world and came to be the dominant mode of conducting "church business." Rectors became CEO's, vestries met in boardrooms to make business decisions, and the laity were told what to do: "punch the clock," "pay your pledge," "attend each week," "go in peace."

The old system is dying a hard death today in the world of business. Should it not be replaced in the church as well?

For a new transformation (Deming uses the term *metanoia*) to take place, we need first to understand what a system or process is. We need to understand that the church functions as a system, a network of interdependent components. A rector cannot be understood in isolation from the staff, vestry, or people; each component affects all others in a relationship of mutuality.

A system also needs an *aim* or vision, an understanding which includes the future. Why are you there? What are you going to accomplish? That vision must be *clear* and it must be *understood* by the leaders of any group. A parish system that does not understand the aim or vision which drives it will likely become little more than a set of competing relationships, all demanding the fulfillment of independent, even contradictory needs. The choice of an aim or vision is a fundamental clarification of values. Jesus provided the church with a clear definition of its aim or vision when he defined the "greatest" of commandments: "Love God with all your heart, and love your neighbor as yourself."

Equally critical is the need to understand *method*. The absence of this understanding is a frequent cause of failure, for answering the question "by what method?" leads us to take action, making the aim of a system a reality. Goals, numbers, and quotas are not answers. There is a need for a method to achieve an aim or vision and to solve the problems which inevitably arise in the process of getting there. Jesus, in his wisdom, provides that method of accomplishing the aim or vision of the church in the Great Commission:

> All authority in heaven and on earth has been given to me. Go therefore and make disciples of all nations, baptizing them in the name of the Father and of the Son and of the Holy Spirit, and teaching them to obey everything that I have commanded you. (Matt. 28:18-20)

If these two, aim and method, are defined well, the system or process will produce a pertinent result. The church is called to produce relationships with the Lord Jesus and with its neighbors. This is a consistent result of the church's assigned aim and methodology. Our challenge today is to keep this aim and method fresh, timely, and innovative as we are confronted by ever-changing needs.

Deming is not trying to replace theology as a discipline, but is rather offering an applicable method for today's leadership which could be seen as a "modern biblical work ethic." His theories of persons are distinctly Christian, and his comprehensive philosophy of work and systems may be one of the more profound examples of applied Christianity to be found in our modern world. Deming insists that leaders need to operate from a basis of profound knowledge: knowledge of a system, knowledge about the principles of variation, knowledge of statistical application, and a specific understanding of the psychology of people and the workplace.

The study of systems is an understanding of the interrelationship of the process of the "whole." Again, we may be reminded of St. Paul's writings on the church as the body of Christ. Paul notes that the body consists of various parts, uniquely gifted, which must function without jealousy and with faith that their gifts will contribute to the whole. Paul demonstrates a profound understanding of the church as system. He sees the church in the fullness of its interrelationships, refusing to reduce it to purely "linear" terms.

Variation is also a fundamental truth taught in Scripture. No two people are alike, and everyone makes different blunders and mistakes. The Scriptures are fairly blunt and to the point about these failures. People "vary" from a particular standard. However, in God's eyes, there is still value to be found within the world. He reaffirms his unflinching love by providing his sign, a rainbow, or more important, his only son as a sacrifice, making atonement for our sins (variation).

Deming's favorite sermon is about an appropriate understanding of the psychology of people and work. His insistence that leaders must "bring back the spirit of the individual" means that a large portion of a leader's job is to nurture workers and provide a means and method through which they can "be all they are able to be." It is a religious statement. Deming says that people vary and that a good leader will know them well enough so that every effort will be made to optimize the system as a whole. Good leaders do not assign blame or unrealistic expectations. A good leader should know that the system is the source of most problems (he estimates eighty-five percent) and that individuals usually only contribute ten to fifteen percent of a system's problems and variation.

People also vary in the ways that they learn. The leader's job is to be aware of this fact and to observe it in action. People are to be valued ahead of the system. This is a hallmark of the teachings of Jesus as well, and the character of his ministry to the people of his time.

Deming points out the important difference between intrinsic and extrinsic motivation. He believes exactly what the church has always taught—that the natural state of humanity is joy. People who work for the joy of living, learning, and making a genuine contribution are intrinsically motivated. People who work to satisfy criteria, goals, numbers, or task descriptions and for material gain are extrinsically motivated. Printed and material criteria are external. A good leader or manager will find ways so to describe work tasks that workers will have the power to become joyous and regain enthusiasm through their own intrinsic motivation.

The Bible teaches that we are born with an inescapable tendency to be prideful and self-important. This is a form of extrinsic motivation. Minimizing extrinsic motivation is essential to recovering joy in the workplace, the church, or anywhere else. All systems of extrinsic motivation—slavery, fear, goals, slogans, quotas, evaluations of performance, grading, ranking, merit pay—inadvertently crush and destroy our joy.

Deming's philosophy assumes that people are more than circumstances; they are reservoirs of joy and serenity, and managers forget this at their peril. Good leadership is personal, flexible, and in touch with the people. Good leadership is merciless with the system itself, committed to improving it so that people can be more successful in their work. Jesus brought mercy to the people and judgment to the system. The Jerusalem Temple was the only allowable place of worship within first-century Judaism. However, Jesus said, "The time is coming and now is when you will worship in spirit and in truth" (John 4:23). For Jesus, people are valued over the system no matter how respectable the system.

Deming's use of quality enhancement groups to identify, solve, and implement answers to an organization's problems have become one of the most widely known features of his management teaching. This process bears a striking similarity to the small cell-group process used within many growing churches today. Again, it focuses on the value and voice of the individual rather than on the more cumbersome and impersonal structure of the system itself.

The insights of Deming's philosophy, applied appropriately
to the situation of the church, represent a revolution in the
way we "do business." Bringing this part of the world into the
church offers a fresh approach to the gospel and its application
to the life of the church. I wish to offer two important lists,
both adaptations from Deming's work, for the needs of the
church.

This list of "Seven Deadly Obstacles" is the result of a
church application of Deming's "Seven Deadly Diseases."[3]
They are factors which stand in the way of quality in any organization:

1. *Lack of purpose:* A church without a purpose is not
planning to exist long. In many cases, the unstated purpose of a church is to keep the institution itself going.
Without a ministry focus and a reason for being, people
are not attracted and the church slowly dies.

2. *Short-term thinking:* Short-term thinking in a church
means a concentration on budgets and pledges. People
give to and support only those ministries they feel are
worthy.

3. *Running a church on visible figures:* Attendance figures at
worship services, church education classes, and other activities are important but are only indicators of how well
the church is meeting the needs of the "customer."

4. *Believing that clergy are the only ministers:* Many
churches work under the assumption that the clergy are
there solely to minister to the congregation. Rather, the
church is there to do Christ's work in the community
and the clergy are there to counsel, coach, teach, and support the work of the church's lay ministers.

5. *Searching for examples:* Churches tend to solve problems
by looking for solutions and programs that work elsewhere and applying them directly to their own situation.
It is more important to know why a program succeeded
where it did and fit it to the particular culture than to
copy it.

6. *Minority rule:* Many churches allow a few leaders, usually from old families, excessively to influence decisions

and innovations. This effectively freezes the church in the status quo rather than allowing it to move forward and meet "customer" needs. Efforts to ensure that all voices are heard is critical to growth.

7. *Risk aversion:* Churches resist risk, even though change involves risk. Churches are rooted in tradition and tend to take care of what they have rather than to risk something new. Generally, leadership in the church is older and tends to place a higher value on stability than on innovation. They are therefore less inclined to take risks.

The second list is called "Ten Obligations of Church Leadership." These are a compilation and condensation of Deming's Fourteen Points for Quality Transformation of an Organization. Their timing, detail, and means of application bear careful consideration. They are:

1. Identify a purpose;
2. Develop a strategic plan;
3. Improve the process;
4. Institute training;
5. Institute leadership versus micro-management;
6. Build a supporting climate;
7. Break down barriers between staff;
8. Remove barriers that rob people of their pride of work;
9. Eliminate slogans and goals;
10. Involve everyone in ministry.

In the past, the Episcopal Church has been referred to as a "sleeping giant." Maybe the "giant" is stirring from its sleep! I feel that this time in St. Louis and the Shaping Our Future symposium may be an initial awakening of our church to a fantastic future, full of pertinent change that is long overdue and laden with potential. However, like someone just awakened from one hundred years' sleep, we need to learn new theories, new paradigms for living in a new era, a new century. This is the present task of the Episcopal Church. It is a tremendous challenge, but attainable. God is still capable of marvelous works and miracles today through the empowerment of his people through his ever-present Spirit. May God bless our endeavors to reclaim the essential truths of church leadership that have served his faithful servants so well in ages past.

Endnotes

1. The Pareto Principle was named for Vilfredo Pareto (1848-1923), economic and social theorist, and states that eighty percent of work is accomplished by twenty percent of the workforce. Pareto's theories concentrated on the power of the elite. In business or organizational systems, application of the Pareto Principle recognizes the value of concentrating leadership attention on those who themselves are the effective leaders.

2. Richard Reifsnyder documents the importation of Taylor's theories into the management and structures of the Presbyterian Church during the early years of this century in his article "Managing the Mission" in *The Organizational Revolution* (Louisville, Ky.: John Knox Press, 1992), pp. 57-61. He notes that the PCUSA even went so far as to hire an outside "efficiency expert" to advise them on reorganization.

3. The "Seven Deadly Obstacles" and the "Ten Obligations for Church Leadership" are collaborative efforts of the Quality Mutual Ministry Institute, 105 N. Plaza Trail, D-42, Virginia Beach, VA 23452. Bruce Nolin is the initiator of these listings.

George Lockwood

A Layman's View of the Future

IN THE EPISCOPAL CHURCH today there are several activities underway to prepare the church to meet effectively the challenges of the future. The vision of our Presiding Bishop,
Edmond L. Browning, has included establishing a Committee
for Long Range Planning within the Executive Council. In addition, under his leadership the council has just completed
Partners in Mission II (PIM), an intense evaluation of how we
in the Episcopal Church live and work. This diverse and in-
depth study was conducted by nineteen expert consultants
from elsewhere in the Anglican Communion, along with ecumenical partners in the United States. Another planning effort
involves members of the Executive Council visiting each of our
approximately one hundred twenty dioceses to help discern
from the grassroots our shared vision for the church of the future. Separate from the official national structure, the present
East Tennessee Initiative's Shaping Our Future symposium is
another effort to help form the church to meet the future.

Our combined vision in the Episcopal Church is essential to
establish God's preferred future for the world, and not a future
by default driven by secular needs. It is clear to me that the future of the Episcopal Church must be a future with Christian
people serving other people. Our leadership structures must
serve that end. The reflections and suggestions of this paper
are concerned with those leadership structures and their place
in the church of the future.

One of the recommendations of the PIM consultation was
for the Episcopal Church to be seriously open to restructuring.

Some members of the Executive Council interpreted this to mean realigning provincial boundaries. Perhaps realignment is important, but I take this recommendation of PIM to mean something much more profound. I believe that we must be involved in a deep analysis of the nature of today's episcopacy and its supporting structures. We must ask what the inadequacies of the present American episcopate can teach us about the leadership needs of the future.

For more than twenty-five years I have been in many areas of lay ministry in and out of the organized church, and have worked at many levels of governance and mission. Based on these experiences, I have reluctantly concluded that the job of bishop in the contemporary American church is an impossible one to fulfill. We expect far too much. In some cases their job is damaging to them personally, and the structure into which we place them often inhibits God's grace from working in these gifted people. Visitations tend to be formal affairs in which bishops, priests, and members of the congregation engage in polite activities, often avoiding painful discussions of important matters and heaving sighs of relief when the visit is over. There is no time for developing significant relationships, and opportunities for solid, apostolic teaching are simply not present. After each visit, the bishop returns to his office to be isolated from the people by archdeacons, executive officers, canons, assistants, secretaries, and receptionists.

Outside of visitations, the schedule of the modern bishop is so occupied with managerial detail that the bishop's more traditional work as "pastor of pastors" becomes sidetracked. Inherent conflicts between bishop as "boss" and bishop as "pastor" only intensify the problems. Clergy and bishops alike become frustrated as expectations are raised and reality interrupts. Something is wrong with the system itself.

It is clear to me that our beleaguered bishops are simply too busy, even in smaller domestic dioceses. One Monday a short time ago I attempted to reach a bishop to discuss national church business. I was informed by a staff member that the bishop was "too busy to talk to you this week, but will call you late next week when his schedule allows." Never in my career in business have I experienced anyone so busy that they had to put off a brief telephone conversation for seven, ten, or even fourteen days! And this was even a bishop in a smaller diocese. My frustration, upon reflection, turned to pity. There ought to be a better way.

The frustrations and failures of our church are not without parallel. The American business experience of the past two decades teaches us much about the present day mainline church. In American industry, the largest of the large corporations are failing: IBM, General Motors, Sears, Macy's, Westinghouse, Kodak, and others are dying dinosaurs that are too large, too inbred, and too removed from the marketplace to be nimble in the whirlwind of change. In contemporary business, there is no room for the imperial CEOs like "Engine Charlie" Wilson of General Motors, who in the 1950s proclaimed the self-righteous truth that "what is good for General Motors is good for America." "Command and control" styles of leadership do not work in the 1990s.

In contrast to this imperial, hierarchial model, the new epiphany in American enterprise for businesses that are growing and thriving, employing more and more people and giving us new and more effective products and services while being responsive to the rapidly changing needs of the world is to be found in those small organizations that push authority to act to the lowest levels in the organization. In these "excellent enterprises," all of the "bosses"—whether they be vice-presidents, managers, supervisors, or foremen—are in contact with the people. They are listening both to the workers and customers, to the end-users of their products and services and the frontline servers.

American business is coming full circle, from small enterprises during the first century of our republic, to mammoth, highly efficient hierarchical monsters during the past one hundred years, back to lean and nimble small enterprises with their ears (and leaders) close to the ground. The church's future must come full circle as well.

Perhaps we may learn something about our present dilemma by examining our early American history as a church of Christ.

At the time of the Revolutionary War and shortly thereafter, the formation of the Protestant Episcopal Church in the United States of America (PECUSA) was guided by William White of Pennsylvania, his mentor William Smith of Pennsylvania and Maryland, and others who were in dialogue with them. These men were greatly influenced by the Venerable Richard Hooker, the post-Reformation defender of the Church of England, and by John Locke, the philosopher and political scientist who was so instrumental in shaping the thinking behind American democracy.

As a result, White, Smith, and their colleagues organized a new church out of "the wreck of the revolution" based upon four fundamental principles: *democracy,* with an equal role for the laity and the presbyterate in governance (but with no governing role for bishops); *simplicity,* with only four orders of ministry—laity, deacons, priests, and bishops; *piety and learning* for those in holy orders; and *apostolic succession.* If and when available, bishops were to provide apostolic succession (for ordination and confirmation). "Superintendents" would administer the work of "districts," and bishops were not to be in governance. The new PECUSA was to be unique in structure and *not* organized along the hierarchical, title-laden model of the Church of England. The first constitution of 1785 did not include provisions for a House of Bishops. Later, when established in 1789, the House of Bishops had no right to initiate legislation, and possessed limited rights to veto actions of the House of Deputies. Clearly, contrary to the beliefs of many, we were never intended to be a hierarchial church.

Of great importance in this new structure was that *those individuals in apostolic succession were to be in parish ministries.* Their primary life was in local communities close to the people. The model of apostolic ministry was to be found in the ministry of pastor among the people, rather than in the lofty hierarchies of the English church whose bishops sat in the House of Lords. This pastoral model, practiced for a time in our early dioceses, gradually gave way to hierarchy over the course of the following century. During the twentieth century, dioceses adopted their managerial model from the corporate world, with bishops as CEOs presiding over ever-increasing staffs who supervised ever-increasing programs with the command-and-control hierarchical structure that was perfected in the 1960s. We then began to be a church of diminishing membership. Hierarchy and corporate organization have not served us well.

There are examples of modern dioceses who have maintained a pastoral model of ministry, and they are examples with growing churches, motivated clergy, and bishops who love their work. We also have much to learn from our church overseas, where so much is being accomplished with so little in dioceses where Christian people are serving other people in acute need.

As part of the PIM consultation, I had the joy of visiting the diocese of the Virgin Islands and their wonderful bishop, E. Don Taylor. It was an astonishing experience out of the best of the early church. Bishop Taylor is a diocesan with fifteen congregations served by fifteen well-educated and well-prepared priests. He is a bishop who is known to most of the public through radio broadcasts, who is well known in the streets, on the wharfs, at the airport, in the prisons, in the governments of the two national jurisdictions, and to ecumenical leaders, as well as in his congregations. He is a bishop whose presence in local congregations is sought and not dreaded. Clergy in his diocese report that "my ministry with Bishop Taylor is the best ministry of my career." The people of the diocese have a bishop who is helping them respond in their communities to human need, as well as to the explosive growth of the ever-present Jehovah's Witnesses, Mormons, and Pentecostals, who project that they "stand for something." Bishop Taylor and the diocese of the Virgin Islands is the closest example of what I understand to have been the model of the early church: a body of Christians who were on fire with the Holy Spirit. During my visit there I saw example after example of Christian people working to bring the joy of the risen Christ to other people in their communities.

Another good example of an effective episcopacy is found with Julio Cesar Holguin in the diocese of the Dominican Republic, which I visited recently as a member of the Standing Commission on World Mission. In the Dominican Republic, fourteen priests serve thirty congregations. This evangelical diocese is growing at a rate of three or more congregations per year. In addition, there are four priests who have emigrated from neighboring Haiti among hundreds of thousands of their people. Many of these Haitians are enslaved at the *batayes* (labor camps) on the Dominican government-owned sugar plantations and are forced to live under the worst of human conditions for virtually no economic reward. I observed the face of Jesus on these people, and echoes of biblical stories were replete in their daily lives.

The diocese of the Dominican Republic owns and operates seven schools with kindergarten through secondary. There is diocesan-wide lay education for over one hundred communicants; for those called to ordained ministries there is a required four-year course of full-time learning in seminary. This is another small diocese with example after example of Christian people serving other people, inspired by a bishop in the model of the early church. I personally experienced every possible human emotion on this visit to our church in the Dominican Republic as I saw the good work of so many Christian people; I wept as I saw the dismal plight of foreign people in slavery living under such horrible conditions, and rejoiced for those in our church who serve so well.

Another example of a model episcopate is Michael Elton of the Bahamas, who each year lives for one week at a time with his people in the communities where the church's congregations are located. His clergy, too, report the finest ministries in their careers.

These are examples of dioceses with few clergy by comparison, with bishops who are integrated with their people and not protected and insulated from them, bishops who provide effective leadership where no one, ordained or otherwise, stands in the way of Christian people helping other suffering people. These are stories of bishops who are able to be, must be, and want to be close to all of the people of God.

This does not mean that I believe that the episcopacy in our large dioceses is not providing some good and effective ministry. I have clearly offered much by way of generalization. The fact is that much good work is being done in the church today inspired and led by our bishops and people under them in their hierarchies. I sincerely do not wish to hurt anyone, least of all my bishop brothers and sisters, but I feel I must "say it as I see it" if I am to be faithful to Christ through my baptism. Our present hierarchical model contributes to discord and frustration, with too many lost opportunities for ministry. I believe that the root causes are in our structure.

I offer here a short list of observations and suggestions:

—Our present American diocesan structures fail to provide the most effective response to God's call to make his *preferred future*.

—The teachings of White, Smith, and the other founders of PECUSA concerning democracy and simplicity in church structures, with bishops as parish pastors, is still valid.

—Hierarchies that are top-heavy with inbred leadership are everywhere giving way to the explosive growth of small enterprises.

—Growing organizations are actively and directly involved at *every* level with the people they serve.

—All of our dioceses in the future should be very much smaller, with a canonical limit of perhaps fifteen persons in holy orders.

—Our bishops should again be required to be parish pastors in congregations where they minister directly to the laity and to the people in their communities.

Bishop Browning is correct that we must plan for the future. The needs of our future require that we change. The grim truth is that the contemporary American episcopacy is not working well. The church of the future must doggedly help make God's preferred future, and not a default future that is completely shaped by secular forces. There are ample models from which to learn—both models of what to do and what not to do, from the past and from the present. The future calls to us from a world much in need of ministry. For us to ignore this need is to ignore the call of God. Leaving our structures intact will undoubtedly allow some good work to occur. However, unless we change, I believe that we will sadly forego many opportunities for meaningful ministry in a world that has enormous human need and far too much suffering.

Tony Campbell

The Challenge of the Gospel for a New Century

I WANT TO SPEAK to you today about the challenge of the gospel for the church as we enter a new century. I believe that though we face serious problems, there is an equally serious and exciting opportunity for mission. In the fourth chapter of John, the Samaritan woman comes to the city well to draw water. She comes seeking to satisfy a basic need in life. Yet at the well she meets Jesus, and not only are her basic needs met, she is also given the waters of eternal life.

In our churches today many people come to the church seeking to have their basic needs met: the need for fellowship, the need for comfort from anxiety, or simply the need to try and find meaning in life. When they come they find these needs met, but also, like the Samaritan woman, they find the living waters of God. Christ has given to us waters of life; Christ has given us waters of mercy; Christ has given to his church the waters of hope, which are beyond all human optimism. These waters changed the life of the Samaritan woman and these same waters, through the Holy Spirit, have changed our lives. It is the living water of Christ that we experience in the sacraments, in preaching, in teaching, in service, and in our fellowship, that makes us a new people. We become a new people of love, a people of hope, a people given new birth in the mercy of God. This makes us a peculiar people: God's people. We care differently than the world and we share our lives differently than the world. That is because the waters of God renew us despite all the pain, hurt, and suffering in the world and in the church. These waters have made us prisoners of hope, keepers of the promise, and the salt, light, and leaven of the world.

You can see these waters in the lives of the people in our congregations. I remember an elderly woman in my small congregation in Georgetown who was disabled by arthritis in her hands, arms, and knees. There were many mornings when I would come to visit her that she could not move out of her chair. Yet, she would always look at me and say, "Thank God for the pain, because my Lord has sustained me to serve another day." Those are the living waters of hope existing in the heart of a gentle, Christian woman.

St. Paul talks about the hope which enables the church to endure:

> We are afflicted in every way, but not crushed; perplexed, but not driven to despair; persecuted, but not forsaken; struck down, but not destroyed; always carrying in the body the death of Jesus, so that the life of Jesus may also be made visible in our bodies. (2 Cor. 4:8-11)

We have this hope. God has given us this hope in the face of adversity. God has given us this hope in the midst of pain and fear. God has given us these living waters in the midst of death and despair, and it is our task to share that with our church and with the world, which lives in despair.

It is easy to see the adversity of the church when we hear the statistics of the last number of years. The mainline denominations that showed steady growth between 1900 and 1950 entered a period of decline during the seventies and eighties. Together, the Presbyterians, Lutherans, Methodists, Churches of Christ, and Episcopalians had a net loss of some three million members. Between 1960 and 1980 these mainline denominations together lost around ten thousand congregations. At the same time, the hunger and needs of the world did not go unheard. There is a hunger and need for the compassion and love of the gospel. People are looking for a spiritual source of sustenance. They have looked and have frequently found it in other places. The Assemblies of God grew seventy percent during this period; Jehovah's Witness, forty-five percent; Seventh-Day Adventists, thirty-six percent; Southern Baptists, sixteen percent. Mormons became the seventh largest religious group in America, growing by some thirty-six percent. The Roman Catholic Church, the largest Christian church in America, grew by five percent. This growth is a witness to the hunger and need within our society.[1]

When we examine that hunger and need it is nowhere more apparent than in the lives of our children. This year, one million teenaged girls will become pregnant; 1.4 million teenagers will use illicit drugs; one hundred thousand children each day will go to school armed, while another one hundred sixty thousand will stay home because they are afraid. Fourteen million of our children live in poverty. One in four of the homeless in America are children: one hundred thousand children will go to bed tonight homeless.[2] In my state of South Carolina, fifty-one percent of all African American males will not graduate from high school, a figure that represents a staggering cost to our society in lost wages and taxes.[3] But each of these numbers has a human face behind it. Each of them represents a hunger and need for the gospel.

A few months ago I went to the Department of Youth Services in the State of South Carolina as part of a review team to improve the life of children who have been incarcerated. When I passed the cell of one young girl, I was puzzled. I couldn't figure out why this beautiful child was being held by DYS. I stopped in the cell to talk with her. She said that she had been physically and sexually abused by both parents and that abuse had caused her to turn to drugs, alcohol, and crime. She rolled up her sleeves and showed me where she had lacerated her arms in an attempt to commit suicide. When I asked her why she had given up all hope, she said, "My mother and father did not want me. My teachers did not want me." And, in a statement that cut me to my soul, she concluded, "Reverend, even your God doesn't want me." This little girl embodies the world's desperate need of the hope and the living waters that the church possesses.

Last winter I was in New York and entered one of those enclosed automatic teller machines. Several homeless people were huddled in the glass booth to keep warm. Most were men, but there was also a young woman and her children. When the Burger King next door put its garbage into the street, the woman took her children from the warmth of the glass booth out to search through the garbage until she could find a few french fries and a half-eaten hamburger to feed her family. The world and this family are in desperate need of the hope and the living waters that the church possesses.

In the midst of this hunger and need we are still God's treasure. We are God's new people: a people of hope, of joy, and of mercy. We need to feel the hope of Christ and know that together we can find and share the living waters. We need to know that together we can "walk on the water." We need to know that together we can be the people of God who can change the world. To do this we must change. We must recognize the time in which we live and adapt ourselves by the power of the Holy Spirit to do what we must do.

In order for us to be the church of compassion, feeding the hunger and meeting the needs of the world, some things will have to change. We will need to change certain aspects of how we live with one another and the way we do business. Change is nothing new for the church. Indeed, the church has changed continuously throughout the generations. There are times we become "calcified" and fail to understand the place of change in the life of the church. Before we look at the changes that need to be made in our own day, it is worth looking at some of the changes that have taken place in the past.

One way to understand the history of the church and the changes it has made is to look at four great periods in its life and the differences between them. During the first era, the "post-apostolic," the church met in small household groups where they could care for and support one another. They were a distinctive community, clearly set apart from the surrounding pagan culture. Roman society was nothing like the Christian community, which cared for, supported, loved, and prayed for one another. The church was something which had to be joined at great risk. However, this contrasting society was so powerful, its love so appealing, that people were willing to risk their lives in order to become Christians.

Things began to change with the conversion of Constantine and the creation of the "imperial church." It was the age of Christendom. During these centuries the church and state were united. The church served and was served by the culture, using the tools of the state to dominate the culture and keep people "in line." People were at great risk if they did *not* join the church.

For the church in America, the third period, from 1789 to the mid-twentieth century, can be described as the age of the "established church." Though officially disestablished, Protestant churches dominated the norms and values of the culture. You can see it in every small southern town you go into. At the center of such a town, you'll notice several things: a Presbyterian church, a Methodist church, an Episcopal church, and a courthouse. The Baptists and the Pentecostals are likely to be further out. The location of the churches is symbolic of their dominant place within the culture. Protestant norms and values dominated the media; there were informal alliances with the state and with economic, social, and educational systems. People risked social disapproval if they were not members of the church. It was to their political and economic advantage to be a member of a church where they could associate with other business people. The church stood at the center of family and community life.

The year 1960 marked the beginning of the "post-establishment church." The significant moment in that year was the election of John F. Kennedy, a Roman Catholic, as President of the United States. For the first time in American history, people did not have to be Protestant in order to gain political advantage and to "make it" in American society. At this time a secularization of American society also began, and an increasing individualism. Churches were marginalized and fell into patterns of decline, accompanied by efforts to return to the 1950s and reestablish the church.

Now we see a new moment in the life of the church. The decline and marginalization which have accompanied our disestablishment are also moments of great opportunity. We have the opportunity to again become a distinctive community. We can once again be a light to the world, like the post-apostolic church had been. This is not only a time of crisis, but of an opportunity to reach out, to change, and to do things which we have not done in centuries.

We can adapt to the new reality if we choose. A friend of mine who lives in Chicago took his daughter to college in Washington, D.C. He packed all of her things in a Honda Civic her freshman year and drove her to school. Like so many college students, in her senior year she convinced her dad that she needed to move into an apartment to help her to study better. At her graduation her dad came in the same Honda Civic to take her home, but in four years she had accumulated a whole apartmentful of new things. Her dad had to rent a U-Haul to carry all of the new things home. Going through the Pennsylvania mountains, it began to rain and the Honda Civic began to strain as it climbed the mountains under the weight. Finally the car slowed to a stop, unable to go forward or backward. It began to grow dark and the family became afraid. They were relieved when a highway patrolman drove by; they explained the situation and asked him what they should do. The officer replied that the only thing they could do was to unhitch the trailer and move on to safety. The father turned to his daughter. She wanted to know if there was anything else they could do, because she had so many special things that she had collected during her years at school. She would hate to leave them by the side of the road. The father asked the officer again for another possible solution. The officer replied that they had two choices: either stay there stuck in the rain and the darkness in an unsafe position in the road, or unhitch the trailer and move on to safety.

In our church we have some traditions and some ways of living together that we need to unhitch. By unhitching those trailers we will be able to move on with God, meet the new reality, and become doers of the word. The opportunity that this new reality provides for us is not only a chance for new ministry but also for new structures. We will need new structures to respond to human suffering. It is time for the Episcopal Church to reevaluate its ministry and to unhitch some of its trailers. We must remember that although sin is by its nature a personal and individual reality, it is also by its nature systematic. Effectively proclaiming the gospel requires systematic as well as personal change.

To become the church we are called to be, I believe that there are four things we need to do. First, the Episcopal Church will have to move from being corporate in nature to being missionary in nature. Our corporate mentality affects our clergy, our laity, and the way we do business between parish and diocese. The average tenure for an Episcopal priest is about three years; that is not long enough for missionary work. It takes around five years in a congregation for a priest to build trust and around seven years to truly be effective. Our corporate mentality encourages our clergy to avoid taking risks in order that they may succeed and move to a larger church. A priest who takes a position in a church thinks, "If I don't mess up too much here, I'll be promoted to a bigger church." By contrast, missionaries take risks and labor long enough to build the churches to which they have been called into effective instruments for God, encouraging the laity to be ministers and missionaries to the surrounding community. I believe that we will have to encourage our clergy to remain longer where they are, to take risks and to set up structures through which the laity can perform their ministries. I believe that the key structures for lay ministries will be found in small groups where laypeople can minister, support, and share their life in Christ together.

In moving from a corporate structure to a missionary structure, we will also have to develop new ways of providing clergy for our smaller churches. When I came to the diocese of South Carolina we had a mission aid request of $100,000. Five years later our mission aid request was over $500,000. The costs of maintaining our clergy and buildings are going up and up. We are pricing our small congregations out of existence.

Our smaller churches no longer have the financial means to be able to support full-time clergy and our dioceses no longer have the capacity to support many of these small congregations. This forces many of our small congregations to beg or borrow teaching and preaching and the sacraments. I believe that worker/priests are the answer for many of our small churches.

A second change that the Episcopal Church needs to make is in the way we relate to one another. In the 1960s the Southern Christian Leadership Conference chose a model of advocacy to create social change. This model was one of the most successful for the church to interact with and change society. It was also a necessary model because there were laws on the books in the South that needed to be changed. The problem today is that the Episcopal Church has internalized that model as a way of living together. We have many groups competing for an ever-decreasing piece of the pie. We have chosen a model which is based on conflict and competition as a means of church governance. Today's problems are not the problems of the 1960s nor are the problems of internal management and government the same as trying to change unjust situations in the world. As a church, we have chosen a way of living which produces so much internal strife and conflict that we can no longer work together. The church has come to look just like the world. To the average person there would seem to be no reason to join the church: anyone can remain at home or on the job and have the same experience. Our fundamental problem is that we do not know how to live with one another. Advocacy within the church leads us away from discovering how we should live together.

A third area where we must change is stewardship, and by stewardship I do not mean the personal giving of individuals but our stewardship as an institution. In my diocese we had a church that had to make a decision about whether to make the complete diocesan pledge or to hire a youth minister instead. No church should be forced to make that decision. There was a time when Episcopal churches only competed among themselves for members. In the 1950s if a person was born an Episcopalian in all probability that person would die an

Episcopalian. This is no longer the case because in our consumer society there is no longer such a thing as denominational loyalty. This means that our larger Episcopal churches are competing with the Methodists, Baptists, Presbyterians, and everyone else. Our churches need more and more resources at the local level in order to do their ministries. Our dioceses need more resources at their regional level to do their work. Dioceses and the national church need to find new mechanisms for raising money. In the diocese of South Carolina we developed a program called Builders for Christ. In that program dollars are raised outside the parochial system to directly support the parochial system. Funds are used to help small churches hire youth workers and to assist congregations in building programs. The diocese of South Carolina also developed the EZRA Project, where funds were raised through foundations to help hire outreach ministry workers to develop social ministry programs for congregations in economically deprived neighborhoods. In the same vein, I believe that our national church structure is going to have to devote less of its monies to program and to direct more dollars to areas that need financial assistance in carrying out mission and ministry. It is my belief that program cannot be done at a national level but that the national church offices can be a catalyst for program at the local level.

The fourth change which must take place is to move our efforts from a weak spirituality to a strong spirituality. Our method of working with the poor has been based on sending money instead of sending people and developing relationships. The central problem in American life is that we do not know one another as people. Immediately after the Rodney King riots our community leaders gathered together to discuss what we could do to prevent a similar situation in Charleston. It was agreed by both blacks and whites that the problems were not in that the relationships were bad, but in that there were no relationships at all. The church must be the bridge to teach an ethnically and culturally diverse nation how to live together.

On Pawley's Island immediately after Hurricane Hugo hit, my congregation and volunteers were preparing over two thousand meals a day, feeding workers in the town of McClellanville. As I walked into the kitchen one day, I saw a wealthy white woman with her arms in a pot of macaroni. Next to her was a poor black woman with her arms in the same pot of macaroni. They were laughing and joking and working together. I thought to myself, this is what the kingdom of God will look like. It will be female and male, black and white, red and yellow, old and young, rich and poor, all working together to witness to the glory of God. We must send ourselves, not just our money.

My hope and my prayer is that this symposium will not be a gathering with no action taken, but that people will leave with a new commitment and faith to call our church into mission and ministry. A few years ago at a football game, I noticed a great truth about life: teams must huddle in between plays. The spectators do not mind the teams huddling, but their true interest lies in what happens when it is time to hike the ball. The world is waiting to see whether or not the church is going to do more than huddle. When we are confronted with sin, sickness, death, and injustice, will we be willing to hike the ball and proclaim the good news of Jesus Christ? My prayer is that we will do more.

When I was a boy, I hated the South because on my first visit I drank at a water fountain that was for whites only. An attendant grabbed my neck and told me that "niggers" only drank in the back. I remember crying and wondering what kind of place this was and what kind of people these people were. But in the South black people and white people marched together; in the South black people and white people sacrificed together; and in the South white and black people died together so that we might be sisters and brothers in Christ. Today, if we are willing to commit, if we are willing to march together, to sacrifice together and to live together, then Christ will be able to bless our church, to bless our communities, and to bless our lives.

There is great scene at the end of the movie *Glory*. When the black Union soldiers were trapped at the bottom of a hill and the Confederate soldiers were firing rounds that were killing the Union soldiers, the young white colonel realized that his men were trapped by fear and were dying. He decided that he must do something. He pulled out his pistol and his sword, found his courage, stood on his feet and charged up the hill. The Confederate soldiers shot and killed him, but his death inspired his men. His men found their courage, rose to their feet, and followed him to glory. Two thousand years ago, our Lord found his courage, was raised upon a cross, and was resurrected to glory. We must look to our Lord and find our faith, find our mission, and find our courage, so that we might stand on our feet and follow him into his glory.

Endnotes

1. Lyle E. Schaller, *It's A Different World!* (Nashville: Abingdon, 1987), pp. 70-81.

2. *Charting the New Course* (Washington, D.C.: Child Welfare League of America, 1993).

3. *Kids Count in South Carolina* (Columbia: South Carolina Budget and Control Board, 1992).

Cowley Publications is a ministry of the Society of St. John the Evangelist, a religious community for men in the Episcopal Church. Emerging from the Society's tradition of prayer, theological reflection, and diversity of mission, the press is centered in the rich heritage of the Anglican Communion.

Cowley Publications seeks to provide books, audio cassettes, and other resources for the ongoing theological exploration and spiritual development of the Episcopal Church and others in the body of Christ. To this end, it is dedicated to developing a new generation of theological writers, encouraging them to produce timely, creative, and stimulating publications of excellence, and making these publications available widely, reaching both clergy and lay persons.